WHERE IS "GOD" WHEN MEN WEEP?

TRACKING THE LIES, ABSURDITIES,
AND UNSPEAKABLE CRIMES
COMMITTED IN *HIS* NAME

W. E. GUTMAN

CCB Publishing
British Columbia, Canada

Where Is "god" When Men Weep?: Tracking the Lies, Absurdities, and Unspeakable Crimes Committed in *His* Name

Library and Archives Canada Cataloguing in Publication
Title: Where is "god" when men weep? : tracking the lies, absurdities, and unspeakable crimes committed in *His* name / W.E. Gutman.
Names: Gutman, W. E., 1937- author.
Description: First edition.
Issued in print and electronic formats.
Identifiers: ISBN 978-1-77143-603-8 (pbk.).--ISBN 978-1-77143-604-5 (pdf)
Additional cataloguing data available from Library and Archives Canada

Cover image: "The Weeping Frenchman." Still photo from the U.S. Defense Dept. documentary film, *"Divide and Conquer--Why We Fight,"* directed by Academy Award winner, Frank Capra.

This book is printed on acid-free paper.

Publisher: CCB Publishing
              British Columbia, Canada
              www.ccbpublishing.com

Also by W. E. Gutman

JOURNEY TO XIBALBA:
The Subversion of Human Rights in Central America

NOCTURNES: Tales from the Dreamtime

FLIGHT FROM EIN SOF

THE INVENTOR

ONE NIGHT IN COPÁN

A PALER SHADE OF RED: Memoirs of a Radical

ONE LAST DREAM

UN DERNIER RÊVE

ALL ABOUT EARTHLINGS:
The Irreverent Musings of an Extraterrestrial Envoy

MORPHEUS POSSESSED: The Conflict Between Dream and Reality

MORPHEUS UNCHAINED: Remembrances of a Future Dream

MORPHEUS' CHALLENGE: Beyond the Dreams

JEU DE RÔLE : Souvenances d'un Baladin

MIRED: LIFE IN THE SWAMP: Ruminations on the Irrelevance of
Truth In an Age of Unreason, Lies, and Killer Pandemics

LES DIABLERIES DE MORPHÉE: Confessions d'un Rêveur

THE COVID CHRONICLES: Once Upon a Time, as Fascism,
Contagion, and Mass Lunacy Festered

LES IMMORTELS

ANTE DILUVIUM

"How old is *god*?" I asked. I was five. "How dare you! *god* does not have a beginning; *he* is ageless; *he* is outside time, immeasurable, imponderable, omnipresent. Your question is absurd and profane."

Or is it, given that *god* takes center stage as the lead protagonist in Genesis—a fable thought to have been penned some three to four millennia ago—in which *he* proclaims *his* self-evident existence, impudently asserts *his* self-sufficiency, heralds *his* everlasting presence, affirms *his* awesome faculties, and warns of *his* frightening retributive might. When Moses is said to have received the Ten Commandments, an event estimated to have taken place between the 15th and 13th century BC, *god* was already, so to speak, quite ancient.

Eons earlier, when man was just a twinkle in *his* eyes, *god* unleashed the first in a series of recorded calamities timed to chastise *his* admittedly "wicked" creation (Genesis 6:6). The mountain-sized asteroid that wiped out the dinosaurs struck Earth about 66 million years ago in what is today Mexico's Yucatán Peninsula. The wayward cosmic wanderer slammed into Earth at the deadliest possible angle, with a force estimated to exceed ten billion nuclear bombs. The asteroid gouged an impact crater about 62 miles in diameter. In addition to ending the reign of the dinosaurs, the conflagration triggered the mass extinction of 75% of animal and plant life on the planet.

And *god* rejoiced as *he* is wont to do because *he* watches, smug, oblivious, unmoved, ruling that what *he* cannot prevent must be endured, and because no one challenged *his* existence by asking where *he'd* been when our hapless cold-blooded ancestors (we still possess a vestigial reptilian brain) were unceremoniously incinerated as Earth drowned under a pall of noxious, apocalyptic darkness that lasted two years.

"Is *god* willing to prevent evil, but not able?
Then *he* is not omnipotent. Is *he* able, but not willing?
Then *he* is malevolent. Is *he* both able and willing?
Then whence cometh evil? Is *he* neither able nor willing?
Then why call *him god*?"
Epicurus — (341–270 BC)

Eli, Eli, lama sabakhthani?*

---

* Lord, oh Lord, why hast thou forsaken me?

IN THE BEGINNING

Men can negotiate everything but their past. The soul cannot remember its former lives but carries within it the regret of having forgotten them. Memory deceives, recollections betray. They repeat everything we tell them in secret. Reminiscing is what sets the time machine in motion. And so the past burst through the floodgates of remembrance, begging to be stilled by the moving pen. Buried memories, those that brain fog or scruples might fossilize, are exhumed from a vast and untidy ossuary. The others, the ones that reside just beyond the threshold of awareness — uncompromising overtones, erotic fantasies, unquenched resentments, remorse, and broken dreams, are slowly being coaxed free. They are in tatters so I pick them up gingerly between thumb and forefinger the better to resurrect and survey ancient sounds and smells and images and feelings so subtle and so fleetingly perceived that they can be silhouetted but rarely fleshed out. Many are irretrievably lost or in hiding, cloistered in the company of useless mementos and unutterable confessions. The temptation to tell all is tempered by the wisdom to say nothing. My memory of tomorrow escapes me. Everything is past retold. In its roots percolates the sap that feeds the future. Past is prelude.

I remember Paris, where I was born, a microcosm from which radiated a larger universe beyond. The address: 2, rue du Pont Neuf. A large, cheerful, sunlit apartment doubling as my father's medical office, with fin-de-siècle windows facing the Louvre on one side in the distance, in full view of the Palais de Justice, La Sainte Chapelle, and

Notre Dame's sublime profile on the other. Across the street, the festooned façade of La Samaritaine, the fashionable department store where, my parents facetiously claimed, I'd been purchased at a rummage sale.

My birth, infinitely more prosaic, took place in a private clinic of the 16th arrondissement where chic ladies had their babies or aborted them, depending on their whim. My father and his cousin, an anesthesiologist, punster, and fan of the Marquis de Sade, were there to witness a delivery that elicited not a single quip or unseemly remark. The procedure nearly killed my mother, a sickly, diminutive woman, who lived to endure with quiet dignity the agonies of war, the sorrows of a discordant marriage, and the affronts of ill health. I would not have survived the trauma of parturition had it not been for the thrashing I received at the hands of the attending obstetrician. It would be my first and last spanking. A difficult pregnancy and a near-fatal delivery convinced my parents to wait before bringing another child into a world now in disarray. Ensuing events would vindicate my parents' decision.

◆◆◆

On June 3, 1940, the Germans bombarded Paris, killing 300 people and injuring more than 600. Two days earlier, the Wehrmacht had launched a lighting three-pronged offensive. Three Panzer divisions, one thousand tanks each, headed for the cities of Amiens, Rouen, and Dijon. On June 7, fearing other bombardments, French General Vuillemin ordered the evacuation of Paris. General Weygand, a hero of the First World War (later a supporter of the collaborationist Vichy regime) directed that children 16 and under be evacuated. The next day, ignoring the children, Weygand chose instead to remove the entire government, *"except for members of the cabinet whose presence may be indispensable."* This decree would later be likened to the spinelessness of Roman senators as they laid down their arms and groveled before the Barbarians.

A mass migration began on the night of June 9 amid incredible confusion. The Air Ministry requisitioned 600 trucks to carry its staff, their families, furniture, and personal belongings, whereas impassioned appeals for vehicles to transport the wounded away from the font fell on deaf ears while fleeing archivists let tons of classified documents fall into enemy hands. Thousands of retreating French infantrymen were booted out of Paris and rerouted toward the south *on foot*. Signaling the imminent capture of the capital, over 25,000 soldiers were quickly taken prisoner by the Germans north of Paris.

Since May 10 an endless stream of refugees had cascaded into Paris from Belgium and France's northern provinces, both overrun by the Germans. The inextricable tangle of soldiers and civilians became an easy target of German planes. The French military had tried to stanch the unending flow and quell the panic, but nothing worked against a bewildered populace distracted by the Occupation and terrorized by government claims that a fifth column, invisible but widespread, had infiltrated and was now subverting France.

In the early days of June, tens of thousands of Parisians fled the capital by car, horse-drawn carriages, even on foot. Trains headed south were packed. Thousands more camped in stadia and railways stations. The stragglers nervously watched the sky darken in the distance. A journalist who took part in the exodus wrote:

> *"We were struck by an eerie gloom that spread out before us at the horizon and which, as if in the throes of a massive seizure, turned the sky from lead to coal black. All of us who witnessed it saw in this phenomenon an omen of cosmic dimensions, the presage of untold misfortunes to come."*

What this ribbon of humanity beheld as it unfurled on the open road were the oil tanks of the port city of Le Havre burning out of control.

South of Paris, the rout created enormous bottlenecks. German planes strafed bridges and fields, leaving hundreds of bodies carbonized beyond recognition in smoldering, bullet-ridden cars or slumped in the shallow ditches lining the road. The survivors, men and women on bicycles, others pushing wheelbarrows filled with luggage, or hauling horseless carts carrying infants, cripples, and old folks, kept going, their backs arched against dead weight, their eyes scanning past the blackened clouds for signs of an impending assault from the air. Half-crazed with terror and grief, some of the women wrung their hands or pounded their kerchief-covered heads. Others shuttled among the dazed, the exhausted, the downhearted, offering hope, sharing food and water. Children cried unremittingly in long, mournful, perfunctory wails. Men, many of them patriarchs, cursed and shook their fists at their tormentors. *"Ah, les sales boches!"* Deliverance and payback were still five years away.

◆◆◆

On June 14, 1940, the Germans crossed the ancient city gates. Replacing the French tricolor, huge flags—black swastikas on a field of white and red—were hoisted over palaces and ministerial buildings. Paris crumbled. A ghastly silence seemed to hover over the once bustling boulevards, plazas, and narrow alleys. Public buildings were empty. It was as if my city had lost its soul. On Place Pigalle, on the Champs Élysées, in the open vastness of the Place de la Concorde, everywhere, it seemed, small groups of Parisians greeted and feted the invaders. Many volunteered their services. Others offered their bodies for bread or wine or cash or protection, or to expiate France's fervid capitulation in a symbolic act of self-degradation.

Weakened by the First World War, France had disintegrated long before 1940. It's not that the military establishment was sub-standard. Its general staff lacked initiative, was short on bravery. Corruption was rampant. Historians still ask whether France was asthenic or whether it had been hoodwinked by Germany's propaganda machine, which had so deftly marketed Hitler's hallucinatory world vision and helped speed up the intellectual and moral decrepitude of the French ruling classes.

Elements of the French army would be captivated by the Führer's fanfare. German cinematographer Leni Riefenstahl's 1935 *Triumph of the Will*, a film exalting the Nazi Party rally that became a leitmotif of Hitler's dictatorship, won a major award in Paris in 1937, the year I was born. Scores of high-ranking French officers, stirred by the fervor the film conveyed, aroused by the gigantic billowing banners and the upward-tilted heads of Hitler's cohorts goose-stepping past his podium, openly endorsed the spread of Nazism *"in counties well behind in the application of such lofty human principles."*

This infatuation was zealously shared by the Catholic Church, whose age-old antisemitism harmonized with Germany's aims and whose support was to exceed the occupier's demands. A defeat of Germany, the Vatican had argued, would bring down the autarchic systems that form the first line of defense against Bolshevism and help the *communization* of Europe. On the other hand, the Holy See had insisted, a victory by France would lead straight to France's demise and the end of civilization. This was an objective to which, the Church grotesquely claimed, the Jews were committed. This assertion was turned to profit by business magnates who believed that the hour of the *white* (anti-*communist*) *Internationale* had come and that only a pact with Hitler and Mussolini could protect against the *red* menace.

Among those taking part in the sellout of France was multimillionaire perfume tycoon, François Coty. In an arrogant and otherwise demented ghost-written column entitled, *"France First! Join Hitler against Bolshevism!,"* Coty denounced …

"… shortsighted, misguided, biased politicians, and the malevolent anti-French sect that serves the socio-financial Internationale and perfidiously ascribe to both Hitler and Mussolini a redoubtable belligerence toward France."

The *malevolent sect* Coty referred to was the Jews, most of whom would pay dearly for this characterization in

France and elsewhere in Europe. The deportation of Jews from France began in 1942 and lasted until July 1944. Of the 340,000 of god's Chosen People living in metropolitan/ continental France in 1940, more than 75,000 were deported to death camps in Germany and Nazi-occupied Poland. At least 72,000 were slaughtered.

I remember watching the boches ["krauts"] march on the Champs Élysées. I can still hear the sound of their nickel-plated boots striking the pavement like cadenced thunderclaps. And I can never forget the sight of Parisians standing motionless, stunned, or sobbing openly, a quiet rage burning in their eyes as the invading Germans—the reincarnated Sons of Darkness—strutted freely in the magnificent and now cowed City of Light. And I will never forget their tears. They still burn in me, unextinguished, unholy, craving revenge. I remember taking my father's hand and huddling against him for warmth and succor. Sensing my disquiet, he'd picked me up and held me in his arms. He'd smiled reassuringly but I saw immense sadness on his face. Sadness and fear.

I was three.

I was four when my father was arrested and severely beaten by the French Gestapo. I was six when ten old men, eight among them veterans of the First World War, were dragged to the village square, lined up against the church wall and shot to avenge the murder of a German officer who'd been screwing the butcher's daughter. I saw them crumple, limp, lifeless on the cobbled sidewalk. I remember staring at the pitiful assemblage of inert, scrunched cadavers, blood oozing from their open mouths, their lifeless eyes staring in the void like those of a doll. I also remember telling myself over and over that I'd been treated to a monstrous but otherwise banal spectacle, a dramatization of unimaginable realism, but mere cinema. It began to rain. The steady downpour rinsed away the blood as onlookers scattered and dissolved in a gray sulfur-laden mist. The butcher's daughter survived the war only to have her head shaved in a public orgy of bestiality and later beaten to death by exultant French freedom fighters, many of whom had screwed France to the bone when no one was looking. And I remember the mournful peal of church bells, loud enough to deafen those who heard it, but apparently inaudible to, or shamelessly unnoticed by, the all-seeing, all-hearing, all-knowing *god* in whom the faithful put their trust.

THE WEEPING FRENCHMAN

Dubbed *"The Weeping Frenchman,"* the poignant still photograph that adorns this book's cover is part of a U.S. Defense Dept. documentary [*"Divide and Conquer--Why We Fight"*) shot in Marseille in 1940 and directed by Frank Capra.

Sicilian-born virtuoso screenwriter, producer and award-winning director, Capra is best remembered as the creator of such Hollywood classics as *"It's a Wonderful Life"* a movie described by some as the Gospel transposed onto celluloid, with the saccharine and deceptive message that *god* is faithful and present in our daily lives; *"Mr. Smith Goes to Washington,"* which warns that in politics (as in religion) even when the truth is out there, things don't change; and *"It Happened One Night,"* an escapist romantic farce which would make everyone believe that this fair country's wide-open spaces, while not without peril, bloom with fellowship and democratic ideals.

◆◆◆

The famous clip in which stunned citizens witness the departure of the remaining French troops after their defeat at the 1940 Battle of France zooms in on a well-dressed man identified as Jérôme Barzetti, whose expression conveys a sense of raging grief so profound, so devastating that it has come to symbolize not only the pain, indignity, and humiliation felt by the French during the German Occupation, but the agony, shame, and powerless fury that vanquished, colonized, exploited people everywhere feel toward their oppressors. I would have occasion to witness the same look of sorrow and hopeless wrath in the eyes of men, women, and children in Paris, where I saw German soldiers strolling along its streets and boulevards, and where *god*, in whom stupefied Parisians had placed their hopes, ignored their supplications and abandoned them to their fate.

◆◆◆

So France fell. The French resisted with reckless bravery or collaborated with the enemy or endured, shielding themselves with indifference against everything that isn't *biftek, frittes, vin,* and *tabac* [Steak, fries, wine, and tobacco]. Everyone hatched his own strategy, devised his own survival tactic, all according to their wits or cravings.

"I welcome our downfall," wrote journalist Alain Laubreaux. *"Victory would have brought our nation great misfortune."*

Those who weren't squirming at such spineless rhetoric were applauding it. Others saw in defeat a kind of divine retribution, cruel but salutary, against a people and a regime that, since 1936, had favored pleasure and ease over duty and accountability. Few Frenchmen advocated open resistance. Many, including some of France's most revered writers, artists, and entertainers chose to weather the Occupation, some in opulence and, if expedient, by hobnobbing with the enemy. All later found the words to justify an obscene intimacy with the Germans that, given their celebrity, they had no need to cultivate. Some even praised *god* for their good fortune.

Enacted on October 3, 1940, a law barred Jews from political office. The next day, an addendum authorized the arrest and internment of foreign Jews. Two new edicts denied Jews access to law and medical schools. Jewish dentists, pharmacists, and midwives had their licenses revoked. In March 1941, Xavier Vallat (1891-1972), a leading representative of the Catholic, antisemitic, anti-Masonic extreme right in French politics, named to a commission on Jewish matters, [the *Aryanization* of France] declared with the sinister aplomb of a psychopath that his antisemitism *"is as moderate as it is enlightened."* He elaborated:

> *"There is a Jewish problem wherever there are too many Jews. Now, Jews are perfectly tolerable in homeopathic doses. But after a while, these interlopers become dangerous, first because they are iconoclasts who resist assimilation, secondly because they scorn those who offer them sanctuary and wind up imposing their will upon them."*

In 1947, Vallat received a ten-year sentence for his role in the persecution of Jews. Released on parole two years later, he was granted amnesty in 1954. From 1962 to 1966, he edited the extreme right-wing, fiercely antisemitic newspaper, *Aspects de la France.*

In 1942, Jews six years and older were required under penalty of imprisonment to wear a yellow Star of David bearing in black letters, the word *Juif.* In July, Jews were barred from restaurants, cafés, theaters, movie houses, concert halls, food markets, swimming pools, beaches, museums, libraries, and sports venues. In December, a new decree ordered Jews to have their identification and food cards stamped *Juif.*

France's debacle and political backsliding produced a vacuum and fed a cynicism readily exploited by flops, opportunists, and small-time crooks who had nothing to lose by espousing the enemy's cause. One of them, Henri Chamberlin, aka Lafont, a minor underworld figure, would play a brief if tragic role in occupied Paris as head of the *Carlingue* [keelson], the French auxiliary to the Gestapo. Driven by gratitude (my father had treated and cured him of a bad case of gonorrhea well before the war) or stirred by some inner compulsion to atone for his crimes with a single act of daring and compassion Lafont engineered my father's escape from Fresnes Prison, where he'd been incarcerated for backing the Resistance, thus saving his life and no doubt my mother's and mine as well. These events are chronicled in my memoirs, a work that would earn me such epithets as *rebel-rouser, flaming socialist, purveyor of fake news, and enemy of the people,"* by the true-blue neoconservative "patriots," and *heretic* and *godless libertine* by the religious fanatics who conjure *god* as they openly wallow in abject promiscuity.[*][2]

---

[*] *A Paler Shade of Red*, by W. E. Gutman, © 2012, CCB Publishing.

A TASTE FOR APHORISMS

My grandmother used to say that *"One of the symptoms of stupidity is an overabundance of preconceived notions and absurd beliefs."* A witty, talented, and prolific storyteller, she suffered neither fool nor whiner gladly. My maternal uncle, a hopeless romantic (and confirmed bachelor—his marriage to a beautiful woman who cuckholded him only lasted a year), asserted that, *"flirting is a science, loving is an art."* An aunt, a notorious adulteress, justified her legendary and innumerable trysts by pleading that *"never to stray is a feat only an imbecile can perform."* My father, an incorruptible man and devoted country doctor who lacked a scintilla of entrepreneurial spirit, warned that *"the transaction that yields the greatest dividends is the one not yet concluded."* Repulsed by fake religiosity and sham contrition, he insisted, *"Better a sin expiated than the triteness of unwavering virtue."* He favored contrition over righteousness. He derided the *good man* as an uninspiring, spineless creature *"too timid to misbehave."* Echoing a Lutheran perspective that was as unrehearsed as it was devoid of religious influence, he often spoke of the *"banality of goodness."* He also believed that sins of omission are no less contemptible than sins of commission because they too involve premeditation:

> *"One can commit a heinous crime on the spur of the moment, ignited by passion, unbridled rage or a sudden burst of folly. One does not abstain from doing the right thing unless urged by forethought and evil intent."*

My maternal grandfather, an engineer and amateur humorist, liked to say that *"intelligence is a battery that can* be recharged only when plugged into someone else's *intelligence.*" And shortly before she died at 59 of pancreatic cancer, his daughter, my mother, in a moment of agonizing self-awareness, whispered "*To live with death in one's soul is to die alive.*" My father cried. He cursed the imperfections of the human body, the primitiveness and shortcomings of medicine, and the savage cruelty of the *Grand Architect of the Universe* under whose aegis he'd been initiated. His blasphemies, which I can still hear, recapitulate the emotional toll that had to be paid for by a man who devoted his life to caring for his patients while being convinced of the futility of existence:

> "*Life is an unceasing cycle of suffering for man and beast alike, and most people live in prudent anticipation of misfortune. Humanity is an absurd happenstance and a calamity. If Sisyphus weren't so busy pushing his rock up the hill, he'd be laughing his head off at us. But what am I saying ... we are all Sisyphus.*"

For all their pithiness, poignancy, and devilish wit, aphorisms evoke what is already there in the glaring light of day. It's the hyperbolic nature of subjective truth that transforms perceived reality into a grotesque parody of itself. But the essential lessons they convey, even metaphorically, speak volumes about those who coined them, or repeated them, about their lives and times, about the ideas, hopes, joys, and sorrows that inspired them. More profoundly, what emerges from their confluent parts is the culture of skepticism and circumspection that favored their survival. Crafted over the generations by members of my clan, countless axioms were already common currency when I first heard them. They may have influenced the man I would become:

> Avoid the arbitration of those who
> claim to be "neutral." They lie.

> Society censures abortion not because it robs it of a genius or virtuoso, but because it deprives the state of a taxpayer and the Church of a hostage.

> One starts out as a portrait; one ends up as a caricature.

> He who walks backward risks tripping on his future.

> Beware of those who haven't yet betrayed you.

> Time flies, but not necessarily in the same direction.

> Always get even in advance.

> If you can't afford a hired killer, try blasphemy.

◆◆◆

Proverbs and aphorisms and in-your-face wisecracks are the legacy of the Jewish people. We wouldn't know how to ride the stormy swells of life or countenance calumny and persecution without invoking some quaint or acerbic saying that warms the soul or chases away the blues, or restores an ever-vacillating faith in divine providence— however transient:

> Life is the greatest bargain; it's free.

The clever repartee that lifts the spirit—

> Live it up. You can always hang yourself later.

The age-old counsel that warns against the spreading of senseless beliefs—

> What your eyes don't see, don't invent with your mouth.

The sardonic rejoinder to airs of mawkish nostalgia —

**If you want to talk about the good old days,
wait a while.**

And the subversive one-liner that encapsulates and concretizes the Jewish ethos —

Believe but don't hesitate to question.

Jews are by nature restive, skeptical. Encrypted in the Jewish psyche, the greater truths and lesser lights bequeathed by our Biblical talking heads are course-plotting aids, not endpoints. We recognize their fallibility. Adrift on a sea of perplexity, we don't follow them without engaging in endless soul-searching or interminable debate. It is our nature to scrutinize, then reject hermetic concepts, to revere sacred truths, then parse them sacrilegiously. *Cogito ergo dubito*. I think, therefore I doubt. Everything is relative, unfinished, highly debatable, often contentious. We owe to this paradox our longevity and vulnerability as a people. Reality is a many-sided gem. It's impossible to glimpse all its facets without being blinded in the process. To see *everything* is to see nothing. So we improvise:

There's a question to every answer.

The closer you get to the altar, the farther *god* retreats.

An ant doesn't wonder why it wasn't born a butterfly.

**Without a trace of irreverence, malice or lunacy,
humor falls flat.**

◆◆◆

By the time I was five I could recite tens of these dictums.

Their origin is lost on me. I imagine each had sprouted spontaneously in response to some stimulus or vexation, all the echoes of the sardonic genius, the iconoclasm of my dynasty. Surely, some go back centuries. Recast, amended, and fine-tuned over the years, others emit a scent of faded modernity. I've since retouched and rejuvenated those that needed to harmonize with the vagaries of my century. I added many more of my own:

Back: The part of a friend's anatomy we can admire when we're down and out.

Beggar: Someone who once relied on his friends.

Conviction: Inflexible belief, generally absurd.

Egotist: Someone who cares more about himself than about me.

Fellow man: Fickle creature we are instructed to love as ourselves but who does everything to make us disobey.

Hope: Antidote against reality.

Optimism: Baseless faith in intangible results.

◆◆◆

I descend from a long line of thinkers, writers, mavericks, would-be prophets, and utopians, each the originator of essential truths or counter-truths that their descendants would dutifully record and trumpet with oracular verve. A precocious ham, I'd quoted them at will when we had company. My parents beamed with pride. When a child doesn't quite understand grownups, he apes them. At the conclusion of a soliloquy in which I asserted that *"The young want to add wings to the chariot of time, whereas the old want to remove the wheels,"* or that *"When two people agree on anything, one of them is tired, in a hurry, or dead,"* I'd pause for dramatic effect and shout, a clenched fist raised skyward, unable yet to seize the gravity of my outburst, *"And where is god!"* I'd first heard it cried out by my father when he learned that his parents and two brothers had been murdered in Auschwitz and that some six million of our fellow Jews had been exterminated in the slaughterhouses of the Third Reich. I thought I was being comedic and had anticipated jovial applause. Instead, as my audience froze in awkward silence, I saw paternal indulgence tinged with pain in my father's eyes. I have since found ample reason to raise the question anew, this time not in puerile jest but, as *god's* absence becomes ever more evident, and with the ferocity of an exasperated adult. Where the hell is *god* when men weep, bleed, die prematurely? Who hasn't asked that question at least once, only to conclude that it cannot be answered honestly without conceding the staggering likelihood that *god* is the figment of a diseased imagination?

◆ ◆ ◆

What I attributed to the miracle of science, not imagination, are the results of a recent DNA test which assert that several ancestral strands stretch all the way to Spain where, once settled in Burgos, my family must have had the prudence — or been compelled — to convert to Christianity, a popular travesty they might not have had to resort to a century earlier. Indeed, under the enlightened rule of King Alfonso X, *The Learned,* Jews occupied positions of influence and privilege at his court. Alfonso surrounded himself with Jewish doctors, diplomats, scribes, astrologers, tax collectors, and bankers. A major Jewish cultural and commercial center since the 11ᵗʰ century, Burgos had already suffered the defection of Solomon Halevy, later re-christened Paul of Burgos. In 1390, Halevy, the son of a rabbi, abjured Moses, kneeled before a crucifix, embraced Christ, became Bishop of Cartagena, then Archbishop of Burgos … and spent the next forty-five years orchestrating savage pogroms against the Jews. He dispossessed and exiled those he couldn't convert by force. Others paid with their lives. According to McMaster University history professor Jeremy Cohen, that century marked a disastrous abandonment of Augustinian tolerance and the onset of modern antisemitism. Antisemitism, like syphilis, is of more ancient vintage. One finds glaring evidence that it began at the Council of Nicaea in 325 AD when Christianity became an *official* cult. Most significantly, this ecumenical conclave resulted in the first uniform Christian doctrine, called the Nicene Creed, a series of canon laws that wrathfully repudiate all the teachings that the Jew named Jesus—if he ever existed—is said to have obeyed, and that his followers then corrupted to suit their own agenda.

Halevy had an able and zealous confederate, Vincent Ferrer (1350-1419), a Dominican friar afflicted with glossolalia [speaking in tongues] and venerated as a *saint* by the Catholic Church. Ferrer engineered the mass conversion of Jews, more often by force than persuasion. He made their lives so miserable that they surrendered their synagogues, which were promptly converted into churches. One of Ferrer's early proselytes was … Solomon Halevy. Antisemitism spread in Spain under Ferrer who fomented violence in towns where Jews lived. He promulgated various laws banning Jews from trading with Christians, corralling them into ghettoes and, so they would stand out, forbidding them to trim their beards. In 1391, he preached to mobs whose riots led to the transformation of the Toledo synagogue into the Santa Maria Blanca Church.

The presumed but understandable defection of my ancestors, a practice widespread among Jewish subjects of *Their Very Catholic Majesties*, Ferdinand and Isabel, and despite the minor privileges or dispensations it afforded them, would elicit—posterity would claim—my family's most memorable and provocative barb:

Conversion is a despicable act of cowardice and disloyalty only a Jew is apt to commit.

Despite its cynicism and distinctive Gutman cachet, this imputation may be apocryphal. but it lingered for several generations in my clan's oral lore. As readers will discover later in this narration, I would have cause to revisit the ignominies of conversion. Of course, Moors fared no better during and after the Reconquista and were also coerced to forsake *Allah the Compassionate* and forced to genuflect before his no less cantankerous and vengeful Judeo-Christian alter ego. Halevy's more notorious copycats would include Spain's Grand Inquisitor, Tomás de Torquemada, the descendant of converted Jews.

The apostasy of the late Cardinal Jean-Marie Lustiger (né Aaron), Archbishop of Paris from 1981 to 2005, would lend legitimacy to the incendiary aphorism my ancestors coined and circulated well into the 20th century. Unlike the others, Lustiger, a vocal foe of antisemitism who oxymoronically considered himself a Jew until the end of his life, evoked hesitant if mawkish sympathy. *"Poor man, he's misguided but not unlikable."* One hundred and fifty years earlier, composer Felix Mendelsohn-Bartholdy, the grandson of the Jewish philosopher, Moses Mendelsohn, was raised a Protestant. Some modern scholars claim that his music is deeply Jewish in character and tonality, and that while publicly affecting deep devotion to Christianity, he never ceased to consider himself a Jew. Converts from Judaism usually justify their defection by insisting that they're now better Jews than ever. Go figure.

The Iberian wing of my family would expiate its impiety (and ditch the Castilian lisp) soon after their expulsion from Spain. It is believed they trekked to Worms, in Germany's Palatinate region. The men regrew their beards and side curls, changed from doublets and hose to kaftans and fur hats, and the women took ritual baths, groused and gossiped, this time in Yiddish, not Ladino. Known in medieval Hebrew as Vermayzah, Worms, was an important Jewish center whose origins go back to the 10th century. The first synagogue was erected in 1034. In 1096, 800 Jews were butchered by Crusaders, with the able and enthusiastic assistance of the local citizenry. Dating back to the 11th century, the Jewish cemetery is believed to be the oldest in Europe. Erected in 1175 and lovingly rebuilt after its desecration on Kristallnacht in 1938, the Rashi Synagogue, named after a medieval French rabbi and author of comprehensive commentaries on the Talmud and the Torah, is the oldest in Germany. The synagogue was firebombed in 2010. Eight corners of the edifice were set ablaze, and a Molotov cocktail was tossed through a window for good measure. *"Where is god,"* asked a stunned congregant, his eyes turned heavenward where *god* is said to dwell. No one protested his irreverence, and no one dared speculate, perhaps for fear that—as all smart Jews know—the question is the answer.

◆◆◆

Some say that if you scratch your family tree, you'll find strands of Jewish DNA in the bark, the sap, the leaves, the fruits. And if you dare dig down to the roots, you're likely to discover generations of reviled *Marranos* (Jewish converts to Christianity). We're very popular that way.

◆◆◆

Soon enough, wanderlust still coursing through their veins, my clan pulled up stakes, left Worms, and set out for Czechoslovakia, Poland, Ukraine, Russia, and Romania where my parents were born and where unfolding events would offer them fresh pretexts to question the existence of *god*, and argue that a *god* who punishes anthropoids for being human and who dares a father to slay his son to test his faith is such an absurdity that *he* would have to be obliterated even if *he* existed. Accused of cynicism and heresy by fellow Jews, my father retorted that cynicism is honesty with a grudge and, quoting Hellen Keller, that *"the heresy of one age becomes the orthodoxy of the next."* Seething with hatred, they never forgave him.

Hatred is an inexhaustible form of energy.

"VENGEANCE IS MINE"
THE UNGODLY TOLL

*F*airy tales can come true, it can happen to you, if you're young at heart. So says he song. Genesis, (6:6), one of the greatest fairy tales ever imagined, would have you believe that

> "god saw how great was man's wickedness on earth, and how every plan devised by his mind was nothing but evil all the time. And god regretted that he had made man on earth, and his heart was saddened. And god said, 'I will blot out from the earth the men whom I created--men together with beasts, creeping things, and birds of the sky; for I regret that I made them.'"

And so, instead of atoning for his blunder, *he* chose to punish *his* miscreation by unleashing disasters and plagues, and distractedly watching as the gerontocrats send the young to die, be maimed or rendered insane in illegal, immoral, and unwinnable wars.

◆◆◆

If *god* is anything at all, *he* is resourceful and wickedly inventive. *His* favorite spectator sport, it seems, is casting a languid eye as humans squirm, struggle, suffer, kneel in prayer, raise their arms toward heaven, sob, and die. *He* also has a sense of humor, which *he* gleefully demonstrates by deploying an arsenal of amusing if deadly cataclysms. Take volcanic eruptions.

◆ **Mt. Vesuvius, Italy** — Vesuvius blew its top several times in recorded history, each time with deadly results.

The terrifying eruption of 79 AD is the most well-known. On August 24 of that year, Vesuvius ejected ash, mud and toxic gases, entombing the nearby cities of Pompeii and Herculaneum. The eruption killed 16,000 men, women and children. Just like that. For no reason. Vesuvius is still active and often reminds Neapolitans of its erratic and petulant nature.

◆ **Ilopango, El Salvador** — The first known eruption of Ilopango in 450 AD is the second-largest volcanic eruption in the last 200,000 years. This eruption was so massive that it destroyed several Mayan cities. The skies were filled with ash and dust for more than a year. The eruption is estimated to have killed up to 100,000 people and displaced more than 400,000. It is thought to be the cause of the global cooling of AD 535-536, which led to crop failures from Rome to China.

◆ **Laki, Iceland** — The devastation of the Laki eruption in 1783 was felt globally for years after the event. It lasted eight months, emitting about four cubic miles of lava. Toxic gases poisoned crops and killed 60 per cent of Iceland's grazing livestock. The volcano released enough sulfur dioxide to cause acid rain and global temperatures to plummet. The eruption resulted in a famine that killed over 10,000 Icelanders, roughly a quarter of the country's population at the time. Laki's toxic emissions travelled south, killing 23,000 in Britain and unleashing a famine in Egypt. Some environmental historians believe that, caused by the eruption, the famine that spread across Europe may have been one of the catalysts for the 1789 French Revolution.

◆ **Mt. Kilauea, Hawaii** — More than 400 people died

in 1792 when searing rocks exploded from Kilauea's crater, sending a thick current of lava propelled by hurricane-force winds.

♦ **Mt. Unzen, Japan**—The 1792 explosion of Mt. Unzen remains Japan's deadliest volcanic eruption to-date. The explosion collapsed the dome of the crater, generating a massive landslide that buried the city of Shimabara and flowed into the ocean, triggering a tsunami 190 feet high. More than 15,000 people perished.

♦ **Mt. Tambora, Indonesia**—Claiming 120,000 lives, the Mt. Tambora eruption is the deadliest in recent history. Tambora erupted on April 10, 1815, sending volcanic ash thousands of feet into the atmosphere. It was the most powerful eruption in 500 years. Upon spilling into the ocean, the force of the pyroclastic flow caused a series of towering tsunamis. Massive emissions of sulfur dioxide produced a severe temperature drop that led to global crop failures. Thousands starved to death in China while typhus spread across Europe.

♦ **Krakatoa, Indonesia**—The eruption of the Krakatoa volcano was one of the most violent in recent history—completely destroying the island from which it rises. On the morning of August 27, 1883, a series of massive eruptions tore the volcano's walls apart. Krakatoa's final eruption was four times more powerful than the largest bomb ever detonated. Its airwaves travelled seven times around the globe. It produced a series of tsunamis that devastated the region, killing around 36,000 people.

♦ **Santa Maria, Guatemala**—For hundreds, maybe

even thousands of years, the Santa Maria volcano remained inactive. That is, until October 25, 1902, when a series of earthquakes caused it to erupt violently. The eruption killed at least 5,000 people, although many believe this number to be vastly understated. The eruption produced a column 17 miles high, raining 39 cubic miles of pyroclastic debris over the course of 19 days. The ash from the eruption darkened the skies of Guatemala for days and spread all the way to San Francisco.

◆ **Mt. Pelée, Martinique** — Until Mt. Pelée produced the worst eruption of the 20th century, the volcano was thought to be dormant. On May 8, 1902, Mt Pelée exploded hot gas and volcanic debris, destroying the entire city of St Pierre. Of the 28,000 people living in St. Pierre, only two survived. Mt. Pelée is active, considered dangerous, and under continuous watch by geophysicists and vulcanologists.

◆ **Nevado del Ruiz, Colombia** — Despite its relatively medium-size, the 1985 eruption of Nevado del Ruiz volcano had devastating results. The most destructive part of the eruption was the resulting mudflow, which buried the town of Armero and took 20,000 lives.

◆ **Mt. Pinatubo, Philippines** — The Mount Pinatubo eruption was the second largest volcanic eruption of the 20th century. On June 15, 1991, the volcano erupted, creating an ash cloud that rose 22 miles into the stratosphere. The eruption created huge avalanches of pyroclastic flows and ejected nearly 20 million tons of sulfur dioxide into the air, causing global temperatures to drop. While only 722 people were killed, the eruption left more than 200,000 people homeless.

Since the year 1500, about half a million people have been killed by volcanoes. On average, every year, about 500 people—innocent men, women, children, are victims of volcanic eruptions. Why?

"Do not question god's will; he works in mysterious ways." Hearing this obscene idiocy uttered makes me want to scream. Screaming mitigates the irresistible urge to throttle the utterer.

◆◆◆

I come from a household where the word *god* was never spoken—except as an exclamation, a verbal reflex untethered to religion (*god* forbid!) or a curse (*god*damn!)—and where death or the hereafter had no place at the dinner table, neither in a mystical nor an existential context. I was never given a religious education, nor deprived of such, but the notion of an invisible, omnipotent creator/arbiter/punisher/destroyer (but he loves you...) seemed ludicrous to me even as a boy. By the time I was old enough to reflect on the enormity of my parents' ordeals, especially during the dark days of the Second World War, their indifference to religion had turned to embittered antagonism—my father's early childhood Orthodox upbringing and my mother's genteel pseudo-assimilation into an agnostic Christian mainstream notwithstanding. Stricken with pancreatic cancer, my mother had endured months of martyrdom and died convinced that religion is a travesty, and that *god* is a cruel hoax. Heartbroken, my father grieved at the fragility and imperfections of the human body and railed against the staggering limitations of medical science. It was shortly after his Bar Mitzvah that my father, in a fit of youthful rebellion, cut off his *peyot*, the curls that had adorned his temples since childhood, repudiated his mother's compliant fatalism, spurned his father's robotic religiosity, rejected predestination, renounced *god*, and began to defy the nearly insurmountable obstacles of youth, indigence, and antisemitism. It was also at that time that he decided to become a doctor, *"to treat tangible afflictions and to snatch my family from the jaws of poverty."* Now a widower, he spent the rest of his days a misanthropic recluse in the company of a cantankerous cat, mourning my mother and annotating the Torah (he considered the New Testament an absurd abjuration of its Jewish roots, and its final entry, the Book of Revelation, the ghastly hallucinations of a psychopath) — not to seek inspiration or succor but to vilify it, to single out the contradictions and underscore the aberrations, to poke a wrathful finger at *god*'s unfathomable malice, to denounce man's limitless taste for evil, to disparage the filth of Lot and his daughters; Jonah's stupefying three-day and three-night sojourn in the belly of a whale — yeah, right; the plot to murder Uriah the Hittite, Bathsheba's husband, on orders of her lover, King David; Joshua's massacre of the Philistines at Jericho; the rape of Tamar by her half-brother Amnon; Abraham's vile cowardice before Pharaoh by pretending, to save his own skin, that Sarah, his wife, was his sister; the slaughter of Pharaoh's slave trader by Moses — *"all bandits,"* he chaffed, challenging Scripture and its teachings, highlighting the lies, the immoderation, the violence, the cruelty, the unbridled bestiality of man, the unbearable inhumanity of *god*. Having long understood that man is selfish, stimulated by greed, and dominated by his instinct of preservation, convinced that *divine edicts are aberrations*, he would seek and find in the ancient texts arguments to flout the beliefs and traditions of his childhood. Pilloried, accused of heresy and, worse, of antisemitism, my father would find in the contempt and ostracism of his coreligionists further proof of vanity and intolerance against which he countered by mounting fresh offensives ... which provoked further vitriolic attacks by those who once called themselves his friends.

◆ ◆ ◆

My father and I often chatted late into the night about religions, more precisely about their chokehold on society. We were not in pursuit of salvation. Our tête-à-têtes were part exercises in pure reasoning and part polemical fun. We agreed that the underpinnings of religion — mysticism, the supernatural, the ludicrous *credo quia absurdum* [I believe *because* it is absurd], faith in an invisible entity, the rituals, the taboos, the hellish penalties — had all been contrived to enslave man, not to free him. We acknowledged the outwardly chivalrous but simplistic precepts of the Golden Rule, or Ethic of Reciprocity present in Judaism, Christianity, and Islam (but probably of more ancient provenance) while recognizing man's inclination to ignore it, nay, to violate it in the name of Yahweh, Theos, and Allah. We quoted from Hillel the Elder, the 1st century BC rabbi who summed up the Torah with the command, *"What is hateful to you do not do to your neighbor."* Plagiarizing Hillel, Luke, the 1st century

AD evangelist unimaginatively pleaded, *"Treat others as you want them to treat you."* Then we turned to the Quran's lofty but similarly insipid command, *"No one of you is a believer until he desires for his brother that which he desires for himself."* But *others, neighbor,* and *brother,* we surmised, have a parochial meaning that, history reminds us, means those of our own kind, *us,* not *them.* This dichotomy offers a disturbing rendering of the three major religions' penchant to replace faith with diseased ideology and their affinity for violence in the name of deity. It also lays bare their unceasing effort to manipulate humans through indoctrination, intimidation and, all else failing, copious bloodshed. Susceptible to excesses, religion is a dangerous eccentricity: it renders men insane. Only religious delirium could inspire a Muslim to plot the *honor killing* of his daughter, to bomb a disco filled with Jewish youth, or order the assassination of a writer they consider a blasphemer. Only rapturous madness could lead a self-styled Christian to murder doctors who perform abortions. And only a Jewish zealot could violate the Torah's injunction — Thou Shalt Not Kill — assassinate Israeli Prime Minister Itzhak Rabin, slaughter Muslims gathered in prayer in their mosque, torch cars on the Sabbath, assault members of a peaceful Gay Pride parade, and threaten violence if the Jerusalem police chief allowed the pageant to proceed.

This is the bare face of religion, a system of coerced beliefs erroneously ascribed to a *noumenon* [*a thing-in-itself*], real or contrived, and beyond human comprehension. This is how religion transforms men into zombies, societies into citadels of intolerance, and incubators in which simmers the hatred of *heretics* — those of us who hold different beliefs or grant ourselves the inalienable right to hold none. Within that conflict rests the unresolved tension between the farcical directive to love one's enemies and the equally binding injunction to reject any alien or divergent dogma. In the final analysis, neither Jew nor Christian or Muslim knows which of the two directives to follow at any given time. By attacking *heretics* as tools of Satan, religious fanatics shift the focus from embracing one's fellow man to the escapist option of waging war against an imaginary enemy. This impasse was the preeminent rationale for a succession of gruesome confrontations in which only *god* triumphs:

♦ The Crusades, which lasted 200 years (between 1096 and 1291) during which some two million souls were sacrificed by *god*-fearing thugs under orders from the Vatican.

♦ The St. Bartholomew's Day massacre in 1572, a targeted group of assassinations and a wave of Catholic mob violence directed against the Huguenots in which 30,000 were immolated.

♦ The *Holy* Inquisition, during which at least 10,000 were murdered. A further 100,000 to 125,000 probably died in dungeons as a result of torture and maltreatment.

♦ The 30-Years War, one of the longest and most destructive religious conflicts in European history, lasting from 1618 to 1648. An estimated five to eight million soldiers and civilians died as a result of battle, famine, and disease.

♦ The centuries-old sectarian strife in Northern Ireland. More than 3,500 people were killed in the conflict, of whom 52% were civilians—all pious Christians.

♦ The carnage during World War I was so extreme that historians have had difficulty agreeing on exactly how many people lost their lives. Casualties are estimated to have exceeded 40 million--15 to 22 million civilian deaths and about 23 million military personnel, ranking it among the second deadliest conflicts in history. Where was *god*?

♦ With more than 65 million casualties (more than 2.5 percent of the world population), World War II was by far the bloodiest. Of those, an estimated 25 million were military personnel, while the rest were civilians. Where was *god*?

♦ The Armenian and Jewish holocausts resulted in upward of one-and-a-half million and six million dead, respectively. At least one million Romani (Gypsies) were slaughtered by the Nazis and their collaborators. Where was *god*?

♦ During the initial Spanish conquest of the Americas, at least eight million indigenous people died, at first through the spread of Afro-Eurasian diseases. Simultaneously, wars and atrocities waged by Europeans against Native Americans also resulted in hundreds of thousands to millions of deaths. The persecution and slaughter of Native Americans continued for centuries, in every region of the continents, including areas that would become Canada, the United States, Mexico, Argentina, Brazil, Paraguay, and Chile.

♦ The 1994 Rwandan genocide which lasted one hundred days and during which more than half a million

Christian Tutsis were killed by armed Christian Hutu militias.

♦ Afghanistan is a landlocked, mountainous country. Since antiquity, its strategic location at the crossroads of Central and South Asia has attracted a number of would-be conquerors, among them Alexander the Great, Genghis Khan, the Persians, the British, the Soviets, and, more recently, the U.S. which, for nearly twenty years, was at war with the truth, stranded without an end-game strategy, and culminating in a crippling debacle. The British lost 457 troops and civilians. The conflict led to the deaths of between 562,000 and 2,000,000 Afghans. The Soviets lost 26,000 troops (9,500 killed in combat, 4,000 expiring from injuries, 1,000 dying from disease and accidents). More than 53,000 were wounded; 264 are still missing. Some 500 aircraft were destroyed, including 333 helicopters. Nearly 2,500 U.S. servicemen lost their lives; 20,000 sustained severe injuries. A confidential trove of government documents obtained by The Washington Post reveals that senior U.S. officials failed to tell the truth about the war in Afghanistan throughout the 18-year campaign, issuing rosy reports they knew to be false and hiding evidence that the war had become unwinnable. Conquerable Afghanistan has never been subdued.

We lie, we cheat, we steal, we subjugate, we kill by telling ourselves that others deserve to be deceived, robbed, enslaved, and liquidated.

As these obscenities were taking place, failing as they did to scorch the human heart with shame and contrition, the *god* of the Bible went after its flesh and soul in ways that can only be described as demonic. And more tears were shed.

◆◆◆

No one was surprised, not my mother, who cringed in the presence of religious people, nor her mother, who considered religion a form of hysteria, when, after having skewered some of the Bible's do-gooders and dissected the misdeeds of *god's* creation, my father and I gave religions the coup de grace they so richly deserve. Branding them *"obscene fabrications that invite ridicule and merit contempt,"* we drafted a jointly-signed manifesto that circulated in our family and earned my father the everlasting hostility of some of his coreligionists until it was lost during one of our many migrations.

We first took Christianity to task, challenging its doctrines and teachings, and surveying the crimes committed in its name, Based on recorded history (and observable current practice among Catholics) we concluded that it is a faith of idolatry (worship of statuary), cannibalism (the Eucharist) febrile superstition, polytheism, homophobia, bigotry, pontification, sectarianism, and misogyny. We did not find anything kind to say about the other Christian sects, including the evangelical movement.

We also noted that criticism of Islam dates back to its formation. Early written condemnations came from lapsed Muslims such as scholar Ibn al-Rawandi (827–911 AD) who eventually rejected all religions and became an atheist. Western criticism of Islam grew after the September 11, 2001, attacks and other worldwide terrorist incidents. We questioned the dubious morality of Muhammad, the illiterate, pugnacious, vengeful merchant said to have founded Islam, in both his public and personal lives. Issues relating to the authenticity and morality of the scriptures of Islam, both the Quran and the *hadiths* (narratives), continue to be raised by critics. Islam has also been viewed as a form of truncheon-like Arab imperialism in which *god*'s omnipotence is asserted in every line of the Quran, and where man's will is totally subordinate to *god*'s will, so much so that man cannot be said to have a will of his own. Islam continues to be censured for the destruction of indigenous cultures, its endorsement of slavery as an institution (which led Muslim flesh merchants to export as many as 17 million slaves to the coasts of the Indian Ocean, the Middle East, and North Africa), its hideous human rights record, entrenched misogyny, persecution of homosexuals, and religious and ethnic minorities, its anti-blasphemy decrees and death-dealing anti-apostasy laws. The Shafi'i branch of Islam has been condemned for advocating female genital mutilation and introducing this barbaric practice in areas where it was previously nonexistent. More recently, Islamic beliefs regarding human origins, predestination, *god*'s existence and nature, have been denounced for their apparent philosophical and scientific inconsistencies.

In the wake of the recent multiculturalism trend, Islam's seditious influence continues to encourage Muslim immigrants to resist assimilation in host nations. Assimilationist arguments are also being raised in countries where Muslims form a substantial minority, such as China, India, and Russia.

35

We directed our harshest criticism toward the religion of our clan—Judaism—for inspiring, spawning, syncretizing miscegenated caricatures of its former self. Our manifesto congratulated Enlightenment era philosopher and humanist, Baruch Spinoza (1632-1677), and prominent modern atheists such as Mordecai Kaplan (1881-1983) and Franz Rosenzweig (1886-1929) for pointing out that Judaism and religious texts foster the belief in and worship of a *personal god* who conducts intimate tête-à-têtes with Abraham, the first Jew on record, later with Moses and the schizoid doomsayers Jeremiah, Ezechiel, and Habakuk, while forming with the Hebrew people exclusivist covenants that disregard and even promote intolerance toward the *goyim* [non-Jews]. As Thomas Paine (1737-1809) so aptly put it:

> *"Every national church of religion has established itself by pretending some special mission from god, communicated to certain individuals. The Jews have their Moses, the Christians their Jesus Christ, their apostles and saints, and the Turks their Mahomet as if the way to god was not open to every man alike. Each of those churches shows certain books, which they call revelation, or the word of god. The Jews say that their Word of god was given by god to Moses, face-to-face; the Christians that their Word of god came by divine inspiration; and the Turks say that their Word of god (the Quran) was brought by an angel from heaven. Each of those churches accuses the other of unbelief; and for my own part, I disbelieve them all."*

"LET THE WHOLE EARTH TREMBLE"

Cold-hearted, intransigent, categorical, the threats couldn't have been clearer or more terrifying to a people deluded by myths, mired in mentally crippling superstitions, and cowed by natural forces they could not explain:

> *"You shall not follow other gods, any of the gods of the peoples who surround you, for the Lord your god in the midst of you is a jealous god; otherwise the anger of the Lord your god will be kindled against you, and he will wipe you off the face of the earth."* **— Deuteronomy (6:14-15)**; and

> *"Let the whole earth tremble before the Lord; let all the inhabitants of the world stand in awe of him."* **— Psalms, (33:8)**.

And *he* did his best to deliver:

♦ The 526 AD Antioch earthquake, the fourth known deadliest earthquake to ever strike the world, occurred between May 20 to 29 in Syria and Antioch which were then part of the Byzantine Empire. The earthquake extinguished approximately 250,000 lives. A fire that followed destroyed many of the buildings that were spared by the earthquake. Modern studies estimate that the Antioch earthquake had an intensity between VII and IX on the Mercalli intensity scale. For the next 18 months, aftershocks kept the fear alive. Several buildings of importance like the church Domus Aurea were in ruins. According to old accounts, Euphrasius (?-545 AD) the Patriarch of Antioch was one of the victims of the disaster who died by falling into a cauldron of pitch with only his head remaining unburnt. The high number of casualties is believed to have been a result of numerous people visiting the city to celebrate Ascension Day.

• The Damghan earthquake, one of the worst natural disasters ever, struck the southern edge of the eastern section of the Alborz mountains in an area that is currently part of Iran. The quake occurred on December 22, 856 AD. With a magnitude of 7.9 on the Richter scale and an intensity of X on the Mercalli scale, the tremors killed nearly 200,000 people.

• Remembered as one of the deadliest natural disasters the world has ever witnessed, the 1138 AD Aleppo earthquake ended the lives of nearly 230,000 people, as per the accounts of the time. The earthquake struck the city of Aleppo in northern Syria on October 11, 1138, preceded by a smaller quake on October 10. City walls collapsed, houses were completely destroyed, and stones hurled onto the streets from collapsing structures everywhere.

• The Hongdong, China, earthquake, the seventh deadliest to strike the world, occurred on September 25, 1303. The 8-point magnitude disaster struck far and wide and nearly all temples and schools in the towns of Hongdong and Zhaocheng collapsed. More than 200,000 people lost their lives.

The January 23, 1556, Shaanxi magnitude 8 earthquake is the deadliest earthquake on record, having killed about 830,000 people in China during the rule of the Ming Dynasty. The earthquake triggered the destruction of an 840-kilometre-wide area and in some of the affected areas, nearly 60% of the population met their death.

♦ The cataclysmic Haiyuan earthquake of 1920 struck Haiyuan County, Ningxia Province, China on December 16. The earthquake hit in the evening with a 7.8 magnitude on the Richter scale. The disaster claimed the lives of about 270,000 people. Nearly all the houses in the Huining and Longde cities collapsed. Frequent aftershocks discouraged people from building permanent shelters and the severe winter that followed killed many who had survived the initial devastation. The Haiyuan earthquake changed the course of rivers, dammed other rivers, and generated landslides and ground cracks over large areas.

♦ The Tangshan earthquake was a 16-second catastrophic tremor that struck Tangshan in Hebei, China on July 28, 1976. About 240,000 people died in the industrial city of one million residents. A further 164,000 people were also reported to be severely injured. The earthquake's aftereffects also brought about a major change in the politics of the region and led to the expulsion of the then ruling Gang of Four by Hua Guofeng, the successor of Mao Zedong. The events were in line with the traditional Chinese belief that natural disasters trigger dynastic change.

♦ On December 26, 2004, at 7:59 a.m. local time, an undersea earthquake with a magnitude of 9.1 struck off the coast of the Indonesian island of Sumatra. Over the next seven hours, a tsunami triggered by the quake reached out across the Indian Ocean, devastating coastal areas as far away as East Africa. Some locations reported that waves had reached a height of 30 feet or more when they hit the shoreline. The tsunami caused one of the largest natural disasters in recorded history, killing at least 225,000 people across a dozen countries, including Indonesia, Sri Lanka, India, the Maldives, and Thailand.

At this writing, rescue efforts are continuing in Morocco following three days of mourning for the victims of a 6.8 magnitude disaster, the deadliest in more than six decades, that killed more than 3,000 people and critically injured thousands more late on the evening of September 9, 2023. As many as 5,000 people are presumed to have drowned two days later when a powerful storm unleashed catastrophic floods in the eastern Libyan city of Derna. The deaths in Derna occurred after a powerful storm and heavy floods led to the collapse of two aging dams, which released a swollen fast-moving river that washed away entire neighborhoods. Videos posted online showed major devastation in the city. Apartment buildings that once stood well back from the river had partially collapsed into the mud. Some 10,000 are presumed missing.

One can safely surmise that at least one survivor in each of these apocalyptic events must have thought, or let out a throat-scorching scream: *"Where was god?"* Or in the case of Morocco and Libya, *where was Allah?* It is also safe to presume that no one dared to volunteer an answer.

◆ ◆ ◆

As noted earlier, I was never given a religious education. Nor did I ever feel the need to ask for one. As a result, I grew up free from religious convictions, untrammeled by notions of *soul, temptation, sin, redemption, punishment, and eternal life,* or a belief in *god,* a nebulous being whose alleged existence and out-of-this-world attributes I found at first more bizarre than objectionable ... and *hell,* which I considered downright hilarious. Instead, I would soon spend hours dissecting the major doctrines, focusing on the aberrations, paradoxes, inconsistencies, and atrocities committed in their name. I charitably conceded that they are all anchored in some exalted if unattainable ideal but found none that does not claim preeminence over the other doctrines, none that overtly condemns the use of intimidation., brainwashing, or physical force to promote it or defend it. I reviewed the fury unleashed among the multiplying cults, the cleaving into *denominations,* each fond of vilifying the other. I discovered that many clerics are ignorant, parochial bigots, that ascetics, instead of facing life's upheavals, are idle, misanthropic parasites and shameless sensualists who take masochistic delight in self-denial and pain. Blinded by mutual contempt, polarized by exegetic discord, Catholicism, Protestantism, and Orthodox Christianity make a mockery of the Christian ethos. Hindus, Muslims, and Sikhs are at each other's throats — as are the Arabs and Jews, all mired in a turf war fueled by hatred and envenomed by the inflexible credos that divide them. Unchallenged by the flock, ignored by the shepherds, such arrogance, it was obvious, refutes the model and corrupts the message.

WORDS, JUST WORDS

Nor did I believe, as we foolishly immigrated to Israel in 1949, that some obscure scruple, some bloodied scrap of resurrected piety had driven my father, a now confirmed agnostic, to exclaim, *"Next year in Jerusalem,"* not even in symbolic jest. Israel's rebirth had heralded the apotheosis of Jewish survival, but to my father, who now viewed religion as a sinister farce—*"faith by force and psychological extortion"*—and nationalism, in any form, as a *"heady tonic for the dimwitted and the bellicose,"* Israel, Theodor Herzl's *Altneuland* was little more than a historical eccentricity and it aroused only mild interest as a revived or artificial ethno- and geopolitical entity.

Whereas I could not imagine, let alone fully grasp what years of religious indoctrination had done to shape my father's psyche, I was impressed, and heartened by how deeply entrenched beliefs can be so effortlessly jettisoned. Heretofore introspective and atavistic, devoid of dogmatism or militancy, my father's Judaism had withered to a vestigial self-view. He would remain aware of the existence of a primal nexus that linked him to the very deepest part of him, but the bond was now stripped of all metaphysical accouterments.

◆ ◆ ◆

Jerusalem, 1949. *Tsena* [austerity]—everything is rationed. We knew we had landed in a swamp of religious intolerance as soon as we arrived. Unable to follow the school curriculum at the prestigious Rehavia High School (I knew all about the Gauls, the Franks, Charlemagne,

Louis XIV, and Napoleon; I spoke little Hebrew and had no knowledge of or interest in the Talmud, the Mishnah, the Kabbalah). I was placed in a French Catholic school where I excelled and blossomed. Scandalized, a group of pious Jews led by a rabbi came to our house to protest what they called the *unconscionable* decision by my parents to deny me a Jewish education. My father showed them the door and told them to keep their noses out of our lives. That did not sit well with the neighbors. They excoriated my mother for doing housework, watering the plants or listening to the radio on Saturdays. So, they concocted, and spread a fabrication—that my father was performing abortions, a procedure he was against except in case of rape, where the mother's life is compromised, or the fetus is not viable. His modest clientèle dwindled to a trickle. We were seriously in trouble financially.

"Nu, when is your son being Bar-Mitzvah," asked some very nosy neighborhood gossips. The truth is that I had no taste for rituals. I was six when I realized I was an atheist. I was thirteen when I told my father, "I just don't believe. Wouldn't it be hypocritical of me to submit to a tradition that means nothing to me?" My father agreed. The neighbors were furious.

One day, someone set fire to a eucalyptus tree in our front yard. It took an hour for the firemen to show up. By then the tree had been fully consumed and parts fell on the roof.

Not to be outdone, invoking something akin to spiritual eminent domain, the Ministry of Religious Affairs commandeered our garage on the pretext that it was unoccupied and handed it to a small congregation of

Kurdish Jews who turned it into a synagogue. I remember them praying to the moon on certain nights, howling like wolves. I also remember them pissing against the stone fence of our house and blowing their noses in their fingers.

In 1953, we moved to a suburb of Tel Aviv where the stench of religiosity was less pungent. In 1954, after obtaining my Baccalaureate, and vowing never to return to Israel, I left for France, alone, and enrolled in the Paris University School of Journalism. The rest is history.

That was more than 70 years ago.

◆◆◆

My decision to forgo a Bar-Mitzvah would be greeted with consternation, not by my parents, but by acquaintances who, like ticks had embedded themselves in our private lives and meddled in matters of personal conscience just to assess the depth and sincerity of our Jewishness. When challenged, I retorted that I found the rituals, the perfunctory protocols, the circular stagnancy of *worship* tedious and meaningless. Such apostasy in a boy of thirteen drew sharp criticism, most of it hurled at my father who, his critics protested should have had the good sense to anticipate and prevent his son's defection. Rebuke turned to vitriolic condemnation when, unable to catch up with the high school's Hebrew-language curriculum, my education was entrusted to the pedagogical skills (and underhanded historical revisions) of Sister Clémence, thereafter referred to as Clémence.

My father had endorsed my explanation without editorial comment. But I felt I owed him more than flippancy or sarcasm. I needed to articulate my feelings with a candor that not only mirrored their intensity but crystallized them as well. First set on paper, then memorized like a soliloquy, I recited the following apologia with equal doses of theatricality and conviction:

> *"It's the words, papa, words not my own, words that mean nothing to me, just words. It's the ritual chanting, the injunctions, the admonitions, the endless supplications, the mawkish jeremiads, the breast-beating, the utterances of indebtedness and veneration, all repeated without the slightest variation day after day to an Adonai who doesn't care whether I live or die."*

I would reprise my atheism, less charitably, in a school essay that earned me high grades for style and a glacial, two-page, red-penned critique by Clémence in whose care my education had now been entrusted

◆ ◆ ◆

Lacking spiritual guidance, I remember searching for an idiom, a concept anchored in reason, not dogmata, a path devoid of ceremonial and mimicry along which I might attain some semblance of wisdom. When I was old enough to apprehend the unquantifiable enormity of the Holocaust, I found in it no telltale revelation. I discovered no occult moral, no oracular grand design in the wanton extermination, by *god* or man, of millions of innocent people, no defensible argument buttressing the existence of a deity so impervious to human suffering that it gapes with serene unconcern at the torments it inflicts on *his* own creation. My mother's death—no, her murder—by pancreatic cancer would instantly and forever obliterate the last traces of polite agnosticism. I rejected as cruel and deceitful the contemptible explanation that *god works in mysterious ways*, and declared that, if that's the case, such mythic being is unworthy of thought, let alone veneration.

Maturity, introspection, and exposure to the works of great minds would help harden this conviction. Often, perhaps too often — some deemed such predisposition a malignancy — I'd turn to Kafka the conjurer. Kafka, *"the supreme fabulist of modern man's cosmic predicament,"* for booster shots of spleen and cynicism, the binary serum that inures dreamers against groundless hope, idealists against pointless fancies. I meandered in his miasmic labyrinths, ready to stray and become ensnared in his inscrutable plots, to merge into them. Kafka would bequeath a lifelong reflex and a healthy lack of forbearance for the meanness, the absurdity, the despotism of officialdom, the odious banality of bureaucracy, of hierarchical structures, impersonal and arbitrary chains of command, the effrontery and intolerance of the ignorant, the shallow intellect and miserly preoccupations of the petty bourgeois, the boorishness and vulgarity of the rabble, the sham majesty of the privileged classes.

Reinforced by experience and an innate intolerance toward all authority, this amalgam of aversions would be steeled by Nietzsche's warning against mindless dictates. What I chose to distill from his florid orations was the obligation to amputate the tentacles of stupidity and doctrinal slavery. Maimonides called them, *"degenerate practices and senseless beliefs."* I read and reread *Ecce Homo* and *Twilight of the Idols*, *The Antichrist* and *Human, All too*

Human, and I dissected and agonized over every word, every twist of phrase, every last convoluted thought until his awesome genius erupted and lit up some heretofore dormant synapses in my brain.

From Spinoza, the closeted agnostic, I learned to reject dogmas that don't make room for speculation or doubt, to call a lie any *truth* that owes its existence to blind faith. Shackled to unbending creeds, afflicted with intellectual sloth or villainy, his contemporaries shunned and rebuked him. Excommunicated by his fellow Jews, vilified by Christians, accused of heresy and apostasy for hinting, too transparently for some, that religion is born of superstition and fear, his was an enviable malediction, I mused, as I vowed to emulate him in some way if I could. It would take a more mature perusal of his monumental body of work to realize that I lacked both his intellect and his finesse. Given the intolerance and climate of persecution of his era, he expressed his innermost convictions with elegance and restraint. Wielding a sledgehammer, I would have to settle for a Spinozan willingness to invite hostility.

Men struggle and fight. They're so busy fooling themselves so that they might endure the unendurable that they'd rather live with lies than the truth. In attempting to rationalize mirages, they dupe others along the way.

Hostile to all metaphysics, Voltaire, the freethinker whose moral code hinges on tolerance and generosity, warns against the perils of immoderation and groundless idealism with sardonic ferocity and wit. A believer in *natural religion* — deism, not theism — he condemns the social consequences of revealed doctrine, calling it, *"pernicious,"* thus earning him the unwavering and everlasting hostility of the Church. There can be no higher endorsement of one's relevance in a world of staggering hypocrisy, I thought, than to attract such antipathy upon oneself. Convinced that it is more useful, if not nobler, to be hated than ignored, I fantasized that my writings would one day be listed, along with other irreligious libertines, in some Inquisition-style *Index* of prohibited books. Reserved for higher intellects than mine, this distinction would elude me. I did manage to piss off a few people and I would take comfort in the knowledge that a tight-lipped but all-seeing secular Big Brother was keeping me in its sights as I added to a rich compendium of waywardness and defiance with every stroke of the pen.

George Orwell's definition of freedom — *"the right to tell people what they don't want to know,"* appealed to me intuitively. It would serve me well during half a century of engaged, combative journalism. But it was the stirring humanism of Victor Hugo and Émile Zola, their focus on the unlearned lessons of history, that inspired me to *tell people off*, to startle the smug and the compliant, to challenge the established order, to prophesy chaos and decay — and revel in all their manifestations — as a hedge against their inevitability. Hugo and Zola, more than many others, celebrated the power of passionate, hard-hitting reporting, the poetry of polemic, the elegance of words honed to sing and sting and move men to great deeds and, occasionally, drive them to infamy, shame and remorse.

He whose only loyalty is to the truth, I would learn, has very few friends. I would long revel in the vainglorious illusion that being friendless is a small price to pay for defending the truth, smaller yet for exposing it. Alienation, jobs lost or denied, opportunities forfeited and, later, threats from some very irate readers, did little to tame the inner rage that consumed me. These hindrances only taught me to modulate the rhetoric, not to suppress it. As for the truth, I would quickly learn that it is, always, the strongest and loudest of two or more conflicting opinions, not facts, and that the urge by some to exhume it is habitually frustrated by those who want to keep it entombed.

In a rare gesture of ecumenical flexibility and restraint (what an oxymoron!) I conceded that *god*, stripped of hackneyed anthropomorphic clichés, is simply inaccess-ible to human thought. In time, and to exasperate Crea-tionists, I would challenge this notion of inaccessibility and suggest that *god*, ineffable and inscrutable, and if beheld as the essence and totality of all knowledge, is a more approachable concept, one that parallels science's attempt to bring all natural phenomena under one irreducible law. I would become convinced, as I am today, that a unified theory linking the entirety of cosmic reality will eventually be elaborated. I would also conclude that, at its core, such theory would contain an irreducible abstraction no less impenetrable than the very concept of *god*, and that *god*, for lack of a better moniker, would be ruled *"first cause."* Elevating *god* to such empyrean status, however, did not prevent me from rejecting his existence and spurning the institutions created in *his* name. Marketing, vulgar, disingenuous, often fraudulent, I have always held, devalues the merchandise.

INTELLIGENT DESIGN:
DAMAGED GOODS

Unable to support their beliefs with empirical evidence, [*"If you have faith you don't need proof*], anti-Darwinists persist in forcing creationism down society's collective throat. They have since concocted a new slogan: *Intelligent Design* (ID), the essentially American, pseudo-scientific and unverifiable assertion that the universe, the humans that blight it, and the upheavals they endure are the work of an omniscient and omnipotent, though paranormal *noumena,* an object or being that exists independently of human sense or experience, and not a freehand process such as natural selection (evolution) and the fortuitous effects of coincidence and unpredictability. Creationists are so strapped for convincing evidence for their claims that they built, under the aegis of the Institute for Creation Research (ICR), the Museum of Creation and Earth History, touted with embarrassing tackiness as a *"young earth creationist promotional facility."* Painfully infantile, exhibits claim to prove that the Earth is no older than about 10,000 years and suggest that man and dinosaurs coexisted before Noah's flood, which also created the Grand Canyon. Also featured are an interpreted walk through the Garden of Eden with a literal depiction of the six days of Genesis, a dark room with pictures of the planets and stars, scale models of Noah's Ark and the Tower of Babel, an Ice Age room, the Canyon Wall, describing how the Grand Canyon was formed in a matter of weeks or months, rather than the millions of years posited by geologists, and the Hall of

Scholars with pictures and biographies of scientists purported to reject evolution. The ICR is a creationist apologetics institute that peddles pseudoscientific creation science and interpretations of the Genesis creation narrative as a historical event. It adopts the Bible as an unerring and literal documentary of scientific and historical fact as well as religious and moral truths. It rejects evolutionary biology, which it views as a corrupting moral and social lie and a threat to religious belief. Its work in the field of creationist *discipline* is being soundly rejected by science but has been instrumental in shaping creationist thought in the U.S. by forcing creation science on fundamentalist churches and religious schools, and by engaging in courageous but futile public debates against supporters of evolution.

In public, ID advocates claim that they are looking for evidence of conscious design in nature, without considering the identity of the designer. Privately, however, they unambiguously insist that the designer is the Christian *god*. [Note the emphasis on Christian]. Forget the *Elohim* that the Jews invented nearly six thousand years before the Christian era and the Judeo-Christian deity that Muslims syncretized and renamed Allah in the 6th century. Pushed to its incongruous extremes, *Intelligent Design* might one day be called upon to quibble about things that fall not because gravity acts on them, but because a higher intelligence consciously and deliberately pushes them downward. Planes fall from the sky, they will say, buildings collapse, and empires crumble because these events are predestined and brought about by *almighty god*. They lack the intellectual flexibility to concede that technology cannot exist without the risk of mishaps: The invention of the locomotive also contained the risk of derailment, the plane of a mechanical failure, the stock market--of a crash. The vilest among creationists claim that these misfortunes are in fact the result of divine retribution. A wide range of phenomena are attributed to ID: wars fought in the name of *god*, hunger, disease, earthquakes, cyclones, tsunamis, and the election of villains.

Creationism presupposes two reciprocal attributes: the existence of a gifted (but unknowable) creator and an exceptional plan from which a useful and effective prototype can be rendered. Such a premise inevitably raises questions that, until now, ID has not been able or willing to answer. One can always quibble: *god* is outside of any human experience; *his* existence is not obvious; it must be demonstrated. Thus arises the problem of *his* abstract existence, a dilemma that lies at the top of the philosophical effort and whose solution has a direct impact on the meaning and purpose of life. Believers insist that if *god* does not exist, then man becomes his own law and the norm of his own deeds; but if *god* exists, man must recognize *his* essential existence and submit to a creator who is also his custodian, legislator, and judge, and before whom he is responsible for all his actions. *His* advent, some claim without going any further, was obvious and primordial, ergo *god* was externalized in order to satisfy the need of men to fill a void.

What creator, I ask you, fashions corruptible beings who kill for pleasure, who reproduce shamelessly, who cling to rival, inflexible, and absurd doctrines? Why do we suffer? Why are we defenseless against natural cataclysms that, according to ID, are unleashed against us for mysterious reasons by a capricious and unrecognizable supernatural force that owes us no explanation? What degree of intellect can be attributed to a maker who inflicts or tolerates atrocities for the good that comes of them? What cunning and irreducible force orchestrates without apparent purpose — or turns a blind eye — to the paroxysms that convulse the universe? What abstract reasoning inspires an *almighty* who remains impassive before the sorrow and eternal suffering of men and beasts? How can such criminal apathy be justified?

What superior sapience grants itself virtues that men can never acquire and who claims to possess equal doses of benevolence and resentment, munificence and cruelty, genius and madness? What skillful *originator* arms himself with an ego and proclaims himself perfect and infallible while our sobs are never heard, while we cry and suffer and die forgotten under the absurd pretext that suffering opens the door to salvation? What supreme entity is it, whose ear is inattentive and whose breast is unfaithful to the crowds that call him out and beg for help?

What *alpha* and *omega* unleashes plagues that threaten to annihilate his masterpiece? What cruel and invisible despot decrees that his subjects will blindly obey the injunctions of his earthly agents, that they will tremble before them, that they will recite prayers of gratitude and veneration, all repeated ad nauseam, day after day to a *god* who never shows his face, never bares his soul, never sheds a tear, never says he's sorry, a *god* who grants life and, with it, the fear of dying? A *god* before whom they kneel or bow to, a *god* who watches them with a stone face and a deaf ear to their most heartbreaking cries? ID is a prankster ploy, a psychological extortion fabricated by hypocrites and charlatans who dazzle and exploit the feeble-minded and subvert them with lies that only blind belief can justify.

As for me, I am never more certain of my origins than when I gaze at our cousins, the great apes. I recognize in their inquisitive and impenetrable eyes an innocence — long since lost in our species. It is when I examine myself and my fellow Homo sapiens, that I worry about the future of mankind. We are a defective product that can never be withdrawn or repaired but that nature will chasten for our impudence and terminal imbecility.

◆ ◆ ◆

The Bible offers a few verifiable strands of history. It is filled with the wailing admonitions of old men high on hallucinogens (or suffering schizoid rapture). It also contains some instructive multipurpose parables, maudlin verses, hardcore adultery, rape, incest, sodomy, murder, and genocide ... and tons of nonsense designed to robotize believers, paralyze them intellectually, the better to ensnare them. The more absurdities and theatricality we are fed, the more we believe in them. We are not influenced by facts. We are seduced by histrionics, gestures, sensationalism, melodrama, and catastrophe. We'd rather be ruled by fiends than angels. We prefer fairy tales to truth, religion to science, apathy to action. When we need to believe in something, our brains turn to dung.

I had no taste for fairy tales even as a child. I found them insipid, implausible, grotesque, stupid. I was already enmeshed in a narrative that left no time for fantasy.

◆◆◆

It was Sigmund Freud who postulated the now widely accepted premise that we are the product, and to some extent, the captive of our subconscious. But he was careful to add that the subconscious is not an amorphous and indelible entity; it is the outcome of countless dynamics, the least of which is genetic. Our subconscious mind is shaped and often perverted by early childhood experiences, some traumatic, and by brainwashing (the seeding of immutable ideas) by parents, teachers, clergy, elected officials, and other individuals who are given some degree of authority over our lives, and further subverted by the idiocies spawned on *social media*. No one is born a believer or an atheist. No one springs from the womb a socialist or a conservative. Serial killers and good Samaritans are shaped, not begotten. The subconscious can be manipulated, and religion is the unscrupulous grandmaster who charms the herd with masquerades that hallow paganism and idolatry (worship of statues) vampirism and cannibalism (communion) and that lead to a descent into terminal psychosis (belief in life after death).

All monotheistic religions are fundamentally intolerant, cruel, vindictive. Neither Judaism nor Christianity or Islam is immune from criticism. Laws requiring the eradication of evil exist in the Jewish tradition. Yahweh is a jealous, cruel, and vindictive *god* (but he loves you…!) Allah the Merciful is fearsome, strict, humorless, and often brutal. Mainstream Islamic law is riddled with calls for violence, defensive or offensive, including the use of domestic assault, corporal punishment, and death by excruciatingly cruel means.

In the philosophy of religion, Ockham's Razor of Parsimony is sometimes applied to argue the existence or non-existence of *god*. Although Ockham does not attempt to refute it, he offers the convincing argument that, in the absence of conclusive counterarguments, disbelief is preferable. I disagree with those who suggest that Ockham's Razor mixes apples and oranges. On the contrary, it illustrates with blinding clarity that a lack of belief cannot be codified. There are no orthodox, conservative or reformist atheists. Atheists do not have a holy book, a catechism, or a hymnal. We all speak with one voice, that of reason. No schism can separate us. While religious people will try to convince others of the validity (and divine origin) of their beliefs, we have no need to defend our irreligiousness. We are content not to believe. A believer feels obliged to share, often to impose his convictions in order to validate his own faith by resisting the ubiquitous doubts that gnaw at all believers. We are axiomatically incapable of experiencing doubt about our own disbelief.

Religions, utopian and irrational, adhere to fictions that do not exist in the absolute vacuum of pure reason, cling to fabrications that must be planted in the mind so that they can lead to certain done-deals: *god* is the source of all essence and reality; Jesus was the son of *god*; he was born of a virgin; he died for our *transgression*, and, now transfigured (?) flew to heaven; he was resurrected; and his death and rebirth opened a portal to eternal life.

Ultimately, all attempts to reconcile faith with science and reason are consigned to failure and ridicule. Faith, notes Christopher Hitchens, is helping to choke free inquiry and the emancipating revelations that night illuminate the blinkered mind.

Atheists are steeled against the circularity of fixed ideas and the absurd dogmas of religion. We believe neither in hell nor in eternal damnation. We do not offer indulgences or immunity from sin in exchange for bribes. We have no pontiff or church in which prelates dressed in purple live in Babylonian splendor. We do not pass the plate, we do not sermonize, we do not fulminate by predicting (and cynically praying for) fire and brimstone. We do not warn against eternal agonies and do not promise life after death. We do not burn books. We do not need a Congregation for the Doctrine of the Faith [formerly known as the *Holy* Office of the Inquisition] which, by its very existence, demonstrates the perilous fragility of imparted beliefs. Finally, atheists, rarely spontaneously but following moments of introspection, conclude that there is no *god* and that, therefore, human beings are neither created nor imbued with what could be a master plan, and that they have no idea what awaits them, neither before birth nor after. Atheism is simple, clear, direct. Best of all, it spares us the burden of useless conjectures. A defective product can be recalled. You can even sue a manufacturer for damages. But *god,* having granted *himself* full immunity, is somehow held harmless for committing the biggest blunder of *his* lackluster career. And men continue to believe in an inexistent being so they can blame it for the un*god*ly wickedness of their ways.

A DISSOLUTE LITLE BRAIN

Clémence, a diminutive nun armed with a razor-sharp intellect and a tongue to match, was a strict disciplinarian, a fount of erudition, and a skilled pedagogue. She would struggle for two years to educate me or, as she put it, *"to deposit something of value in this untidy, dissolute little brain of yours."*

The encyclopedic knowledge that Clémence possessed — she'd been licensed to teach everything from algebra to zoology — was often overshadowed by an appalling lack of objectivity. It was the very richness of her scholarship that enabled her, whenever the occasion arose, to skew history or to rewrite it by opining unabashedly about people long dead or by editorializing about events exhaustively evidenced and chronicled in the otherwise unembellished secular French government curriculum she was required to follow. A royalist, as are all devout French Catholics, she steadfastly justified the arrogance and cruelty of French monarchs by pleading that they were, after all, *"bons catholiques."* It is true that many among them spent time genuflecting in their private gilded chapels on ermine stoles and rich brocades while their vassals lived in squalor, starved, and died of the plague. Distant abstractions, the Crusades and the *Holy* Inquisition elicited a kind of nostalgic admiration stripped of all compunction for the horrors committed in their name.

I remember learning about the events that took place on the night of August 23, 1572, better known as the Saint-

Bartholomew massacre, during which 3,000 Protestants were slaughtered in the streets of Paris on order of Catherine de Medici. Reviewing the incident did not seem to evoke in my teacher any discernible unease. (News of the incident had been cheered by Spain's dementedly devout Philip II, himself busy purging Spain of Protestants, Jews, and Moors, and Pope Gregory XIII, who celebrated a *Te Deum* mass to commemorate the blessed events and who, for lack of better things to do, reformed the calendar).

It was at that time that began germinating in me the notion that the Inquisition, as an ethos and instrument of statecraft, did not expire in the bonfires of the Dark Ages but persisted and mutated into a ghoulish instrument of racism, colonization, slavery, segregation, wars of imperialism (territorial, political, and religious) and the curtailment of civil rights in times of internal strife. Future events, some of which I would write about, among them the assassination of Central American street children by police, and the state-sponsored persecution of indigenous minorities, would help crystallize this insight. I would later discover that distinguished historian, Jacques Barzun (1907-2012), writing in *From Dawn to Decadence*, had far more eloquently reached the same conclusions:

> *"The many dictatorships of the 20th century have relied on [the Inquisition] and in free countries it thrives ad hoc – hunting down German sympathizers during the First World War, interning Japanese-Americans during the second, and pursuing 'communist' fellow-travelers during the Cold War. In the United States, the workings of 'political correctness' in universities and the speech police*

that punishes persons and corporations for words on certain topics quaintly called 'sensitive' are manifestations of the permanent spirit of Inquisition. "

The climate of fear and suspicion that befell America following the tragic events of September 11, 2001 — during which 3,000 people perished, among them 343 firemen — and while *Yahweh, Theos,* and *Allah* were conspicuously absent, would lend credence to the notion that the inquisitorial spirit, dormant at times of tranquility, will be speedily aroused in times of turmoil. To its immense credit, the U.S., while vigilant, did not succumb to wholesale paranoia — or at least did not openly admit to doing so as it secretly began to snoop into the lives of private citizens and launched yet another undeclared, illegal, immoral, and unwinnable war, this time premised on the fake pretext that Saddam Hussein, who had been Our Man in Baghdad, was amassing weapons of mass destruction.

Half a century earlier, injecting personal bias into her instructions, Clémence presided over her own kangaroo court. She scorned the Huguenot Henri of Navarre but lavished him with gushing praise when, crowned Henri IV and fearful for his neck, he converted to Catholicism. *"Paris vaut bien une messe."* [Paris is well worth a Mass]. Praise turned to condemnation yet again when the good king, now firmly enthroned, issued the Edict of Nantes, a decree restoring religious and political rights to French Protestants. A few chapters forward, my teacher applauded the Edict's revocation, 87 years later, by the *Sun King* Louis XIV, the archetype war-mongering despot whose arrogance was eclipsed only by his flamboyance.

Unaware of or utterly indifferent to the immense suffering of their subjects, Louis XVI, who spent his reign tinkering with clocks, and his wife, Marie-Antoinette, who plundered France coffers to keep the court royally entertained (while financing America's war of independence) elicited pity and sympathy from Clémence:

"Ils étaient très pieux et se recueillaient en prière plusieurs fois par jour," she intoned, exculpating the pair because *"they were very pious and gathered in prayer several times a day."* As these enormities were being casually spouted, I would retrieve from the depths of childhood memories images of priests sprinkling *holy water* on tanks and cannons and the fuselage of dive bombers so that Christians could kill and maim other Christians with the full blessings of almighty *god.*

My impious rejoinders, smack dab in the middle of history class would elicit stern, if ornate, reminders of *god's* irrefutability:

"Between god and us," sermonized the irate nun, *"rises a tall, impenetrable glass partition, transparent for him, opaque for us; he does not reveal himself. We wouldn't recognize him if he did. To be found, he must be discovered."*

"Discovered? Discovered?" I would retort. "Logic suggests that what doesn't exist can't be discovered. If *god,* invented by man, really existed, wouldn't *he* have been by now discovered, substantiated?"

To which Clémence haughtily replied, *"god grants us some of his spirit but will never reveal his logic."*

What I would learn from these verbal skirmishes and

artful equivocations is that *god* might be no more than a tenuous hypothesis to some, *he*'s indispensable to many others. Troubled by the subconscious fear that logic might dim *his* existence, they cling even harder to their beliefs.

Knowledge discredits myths:
faith reinforces them.

◆◆◆

The French Revolution, Clémence would have her class believe, was *"an outrage masterminded by money lenders* [translation: Jews] *Freemasons* [the perennial target of the Church], and *"degenerate philosophers."* This characterization was nowhere to be found in the history text we'd been issued. It's interesting to note that in reading passages from the works of Diderot, Montesquieu, Rousseau, and Voltaire [the leading 18th century *degenerate* French thinkers], we were encouraged to emulate their elegant literary style, but enjoined from embracing their *"amoral, irreligious, licentious"* ideas.

The reign of terror that followed the fall of the Bastille on July 14, 1789, was summarily blasted as a *"grotesque act of barbarism against Christian values."* Yes, many innocent heads rolled during the two-year frenzy. But Clémence could not bring herself to view the insurrection as the cathartic articulation of centuries of misery and oppression or as the impetus that would help rid France, for the first time in its history from the yoke of feudalism, absolute monarchy, and stifling theocratic control. The assassination in his bathtub, in 1793, of Jean-Paul Marat, a popular physician, lawyer, journalist, and legislator, would be glibly dismissed as *"the elimination of a scoundrel by a brave Catholic young woman."* Charlotte Corday, of noble birth, would later pay for her crime on the guillotine. In contrast, the beheading of two royal idlers who bankrupted France while they wined, dined, gambled, gathered piously in prayer, and unleashed their dogs on helpless foxes, Clémence insisted, was murder. Nor did she seem to understand that revolution is a process, not a single incident. The burgeoning concepts of human rights,, equality, suffrage, and the abolition of monarchy actually took root one hundred years before the storming of the famous landmark prison fortress. In a letter to Louis XIV, François Fénelon, the king's almoner had warned:

> *"Sire, for thirty years your ministers have violated all the ancient laws in the state so as to enhance your power. They have increased your revenues and your expenditures to the infinite and impoverished all of France for the sake of your luxury at court. They have made your name odious. For twenty years they have made the French nation intolerable to its neighbors by bloody wars. We have no allies because we only wanted slaves. Meanwhile, your people are starving. Sedition is spreading and you are reduced to either letting it spread unpunished or resorting to massacring the people that you have driven to desperation."*

A sharp critic of the monarchy, the very politically incorrect Fénelon was fired by the Sun King for uttering truths the king did not want to hear. Less than one hundred years later, the long simmering embers of misery and discontent ignited the Revolution. Two centuries later, George Orwell would define freedom as the right to tell people what they don't want to know.

The French Revolution was an extraordinarily

complicated affair rooted in centuries of mismanagement, extravagance and war, and ignited by the rising friction between the three Estates—a bloated, do-nothing, hedonistic aristocracy, a debauched clergy, and a crushing mass of dirt-poor, illiterate and downtrodden serfs. The *"nobility of the sword"*—500,000-strong, consisted of hangers-on and sycophants; the petty nobility, composed of provincial families of lesser means but matching greed and ambition; and the nouveaux-riche, the *parvenus*—people of obscure origin who acquired wealth, influence, or celebrity, often by less than honorable means—who bought nobility titles and who, despite their wealth, were scorned by the traditional bluebloods for their miserly origins. Next was the ecclesiastical class—120,000 men of the cloth, among them the high clergy (members of the aristocracy) and the common clerics—all depraved. Last was the Third Estate, the populace representing the proletariat—day-workers, farmers, peasants, craftsmen, and the bourgeoisie—bankers, lawyers and trades people.

This was the twilight of the 18th century, the era of Enlightenment, and France was tired of the ancient and traditional monarchical order in which the king was commander in chief, judge, jury and, often, executioner, and wary of a system that called for the nobility to defend the nation (make war), the clergy to pray for victory, and the rabble to pay crippling levies and labor until they dropped. The clergy paid no taxes but charged tolls on behalf of the Crown, and sold indulgences and first-class passage to heaven, with much of the monies diverted and adding to the personal fortunes of the Princes of the Church.

My teacher should have known all that. She probably did but she never allowed fact to interfere with her faith. As Nietzsche famously said, *"Faith means not wanting to know what is true."*

◆◆◆

Conceding that Napoleon was brilliant, ruthless, lustful, utopian, and flawed, Clémence glossed over his triumphs, the idealism of his social reforms, his patronage of the arts, sciences, education, and jurisprudence, but ranted about his *"impiety and vanity, sins even a great man can never expiate."* She was referring to an incident during his coronation as emperor of France, when Bonaparte, *"shamelessly and sacrilegiously"* yanked the crown from the Pope's hands and placed it on his head. There was something offensive about the petty vilification of a man praised for his genius, if not always for the wisdom of his geopolitical objectives.

Outspoken, my teacher's antipathy toward fellow Christians — she scorned Protestants, mocked the Greek and Russian Orthodox faith, sneered at the *lesser cults* of Copts and Maronites — assumed subtler hues when it came to Jews. Her brand of antisemitism was ill-defined and furtive, tempered no doubt by the persuasive political realities of the day. The school was now seated in Israel, not Palestine, as it had been two years earlier. Moreover, four-fifths of the students were Jewish. I did not feel threatened. Wary of beliefs that defy verifiable fact, intuitively aware that the role of a school is to ossify young minds (I'd already been exposed to the crude encoding methods of *communist* pedagogy in Romania) I didn't take these digressions too seriously because they afforded me an opportunity to refute them. Instead, I learned to beware of opinions — hand-me-down convictions difficult or impossible to temper and often adopted in defiance of their glaring flaws. Besides, I had enough trouble keeping up with schoolwork, and whatever reflex contempt Christians have for *"Christ's killers"* it did not seem to be directed at me personally. Clémence was in fact quite fond of her students. I would be less than honest if I did not acknowledge a measure of esteem for her patience and forbearance, and gratitude for every snippet of knowledge she managed to instill, including--inadvertently perhaps--the art of confutation. Esteem did not prevent me from challenging her on occasion and standing my ground until she relented or changed the subject.

◆◆◆

Learning about (in my case reexamining) the Dreyfus Affair, gave rise to such occasion. I was ready. I had read a great deal about it and my father, who had studied the case in great depth, had helped sort documented fact from idle talk and deliberate disinformation. The Affair aroused passions and prejudices that divided France and very nearly triggered a civil war. An epic of lies, treachery, intimidation, fraud, and injustice, it revived and widened the philosophical rifts that polarize societies in times of unrest and discontent-- the right against the left, the rich against the proletariat, the clerical elite against the secular masses, the military against the constitutionally elected civilian regimes, the fascists against the Jews, Blacks, Hispanic, and Asians, the Church against liberals and freethinkers. The same antithetical ideologies that polarized the French during the 1789 Revolution, the German Occupation, and the wars in Algeria and Indochina, would lead to the alarming ascent in the 20th century of ultra-conservatism, xenophobia, and religious fanaticism.

The Dreyfus Affair began as a banal case of espionage. On September 26, 1894, the French Bureau of Statistics learned of a memorandum purloined from the German Embassy in Paris attesting to the presence of a traitor in France's military high command. Suspicions fell on a young French officer, Captain Alfred Dreyfus, whose race — he was Jewish — offered a military establishment noted more for its antisemitism than its prowess on the battlefield the pretext it had been looking for. Two weeks later, on very flimsy evidence (later to be proven fake), and with the tacit approval of the Catholic Church, Dreyfus was arrested. French War Minister Auguste Mercier, chiefs of staff, and high-ranking political figures, aware of the plot against Dreyfus, pressed on for a speedy trial. Dreyfus was found guilty and sentenced to life imprisonment in a *"fortified compound,"* a sinister euphemism for the hell hole that Guyana's Devil's Island would prove to be. On January 5, 1895, Dreyfus was publicly stripped of his rank and his saber was broken in half as crowds chanted, *"Death to the Jews! Death to the traitor! Death to Judas!"* Having barely survived five years of incarceration in one of the most infamous penal colonies, Dreyfus was returned to France in 1900, pardoned, reinstated by the Supreme Court in 1902, and promoted to colonel, largely thanks to Émile Zola's tireless efforts on his behalf. The celebrated novelist and social critic had written a scathing open letter, the famed

"J'Accuse...!" published on the front page of the newspaper *L'Aurore* [Dawn] in which Zola targeted French president, Félix Faure, accused his government of antisemitism, denounced Dreyfus' unlawful jailing and cited grave judicial errors. The letter caused disturbances in France and abroad. Zola was prosecuted for libel and found guilty in 1898. To avoid imprisonment, he fled to England, returning home in June 1899.

The government had first offered Dreyfus a plea deal—a pardon rather than an exoneration, which he could accept and go free, thus effectively admitting guilt, or face a retrial at which he was sure to be re-convicted. Although he was clearly innocent, he chose to accept the pardon.

Zola died in Paris in 1902 of carbon monoxide poisoning allegedly caused by a malfunctioning chimney flue. He was 62 and had been in perfect health. There is circumstantial evidence suggesting that he may have been assassinated by political foes. Dreyfus, who attended Zola's funeral at Les Invalides, was shot and wounded by a man who, despite witness accounts of the crime, was cleared in court. Unmoved by a growing wave of revulsion sweeping France, most politicians and prominent Church figures continued to insinuate that Dreyfus was guilty, or aligned themselves with factions opposed to his rehabilitation in the court of public opinion. Fresh rumors would perpetuate and legitimize ill will toward the officer's defenders. Centuries of religious struggles had unsurprisingly produced much cynicism and distrust toward religion in France. The Dreyfus Affair epitomized the conflict between clerical/monarchist and anticlerical/republican forces.

❖ ❖ ❖

"Yes," Clémence orated, "the Freemasons engineered his release. But his innocence was never really proven and..."

This was an abject fabrication. What she had no way of knowing (or may have deliberately overlooked) is that Masonic lodges, not quite ready to open their doors to Jews, had conveniently retreated behind their statutory shield during the Affair. The Anderson Constitution, the founding principles and tenets of Freemasonry, proclaims that Freemasons are law-abiding citizens who do not meddle in the affairs of state. Sympathizing with Dreyfus, let alone intervening on his behalf, would have violated Masonic protocols, rekindled the Church's age-old antisemitism, and reanimated its seething hatred of the Masons. Thus the fraternity not only failed to intervene, but it also responded with cowardice and irresolution in the face of gross injustice, And the *Widow's Son* was immolated yet again at the altar of political expediency.

"What about the forgeries by the French chiefs of staff," I interjected. "What about Count Esterhazy," a name absent from my history book. "What about his jailhouse confession?" Clémence smiled with unease.

"Well, that proves nothing. Other facts ..."

"O.K. What about '*Le Lion?'*" The mighty Georges Clemenceau, twice-prime minister of France and fierce advocate of the separation of church and state had roared with outrage at Dreyfus' arrest and incarceration. The great Zola had thundered and exhorted France to look at itself. And the entire French military high command had been accused of conspiring to pin an act of high treason on an innocent man, a Jewish officer. *"None of this is spelled out in here,"* I cried out, tapping repeatedly the history book with my forefinger. "What other facts?"

I don't remember ever getting a straight answer.

◆◆◆

It is hard for schoolchildren to extricate fact from fancy. Teachers, venerated professionals when I was a boy can add to the confusion. Depending on our intuition, knowledge of facts, and common sense, we see them as champions of Solomonic wisdom or purveyors of deception. We marvel at their erudition or dismiss their asides as the views of demagogues prone to scuttle the truth. It is when they resort to calumny, when they trivialize or repudiate reality with outlandish allegations, and when grotesque beliefs color their opinions that the truth drowns.

◆◆◆

Clémence must have known that I would be a handful when she accepted to enroll me in her all-girls' school. Endless pranks, habitual insubordination, and a barrage of firebrand compositions, I'm sure, had earned her a place in the tabernacle of saints. What she may not have anticipated were the raging hormones and the premature onset of puberty that transform an otherwise likable little rascal into un *enfant terrible* whose evolving interest in the opposite gender is apt to mutate into socially unacceptable mischief. Clémence would eventually arrange to have me transferred to an all-boys' school.

◆◆◆

71

History may be a long march, but life is a short stroll on a very narrow, slippery footpath. The road from Jerusalem to Jaffa where my new school was located was littered with the mementos of war: A charred, overturned bus; a mutilated armored troop carrier resting on its side like a wounded beast on a desolate bluff; a tank, its turret gaping like an open wound, its tracks severed and caked with mud, its once deadly cannon truncated, its flanks etched with graffiti — initials, cryptic verses, arrowed hearts, words of love and sorrow for fallen heroes and words of peace and hope for an infant nation bleeding as it took its first breath. The spectacle would also inspire lasting feelings about the folly of war, the fragility of life, the lunatic ambivalence of the human spirit, and, most noticeably, the absence of divine compassion.

CARDINAL SINS:
LIBERATION THEOLOGY SHACKLED

Newsmen don't live by fact alone. Fact may be the backbone of a story that can be told with the essential *who, what, when, where, and how*. But there's a latticework of nerve and sinew and flesh—the *why* or *why not* of an event or issue—that begs to be dissected and bared because such postmortem helps advance the cause of truth. Bringing into focus the shadowy forces and peripheral influences that shape history, stirring the slime that percolates hidden from view is the duty of honest journalism. But doing so invites accusations of muckraking, rabble-rousing, and radicalism, laudable labels that *mainstream* journalists work hard not to earn. Such timidity, driven by tacit covenants with, or pressure from, political and faith-based groups—not scruples— often leads to selective coverage and results in hasty inferences slanted to conform to the orthodoxy of the moment. In the current climate of political correctness, intemperate nationalism, and off-the-wall religious fervor, this pusillanimity also tends to corrupt the journalist.

Working in Central America, as I did for twelve years, would offer me unparalleled opportunities to break some taboos (exposing U.S. crimes in the Isthmus) and defy the canons of sanctioned reporting (ignoring my editors' injunction to *"lay off"* certain subjects) not out of concern for my safety but to protect their publications from legal entanglements. I'd long resolved to serve no master. I would neither pay lip service to official propaganda, nor would I obey the conditions imposed by some of the papers for which I freelanced. In time, emboldened by the acrimony that my investigative reports and commentaries inspired, seduced by the effect they had on readers, I would take on some of history's more sinister sideshows. One was the incestuous relationship between the Catholic Church and political and military power structures, that grotesque symbiosis during which the high clergy, politicians, and bemedaled colonels intersect, merge, and feed on each other. The other was the destabilizing consequences of U.S. military adventurism in that region. The perfidious war waged by the Vatican against Liberation Theology and the wasteland of death and destruction left by alumni of the U.S. Army School of the Americas (since blandly rechristened the Western Hemisphere Institute for Security Cooperation).

◆◆◆

In appointing arch-conservative Bishop Fernando Saenz Lacalle (1932-2022) to succeed slain Salvadoran Archbishop Oscar Romero*, Pope John Paul II, then on a whirlwind tour of El Salvador, Guatemala, Nicaragua, and Venezuela, struck hard at the Theology of Liberation, the oxygen-rich doctrine that redefined and, for the poor and voiceless, enlivened Roman Catholicism in Latin America in the preceding fifty years.

Predictably, in a region bled dry by war, weakened by economic decay, and enfeebled by harsh austerity measures, the Pope's choice came as a shock and

---

* Col. Roberto d'Aubuisson (1943-1992) Salvadoran neo-fascist death-squad leader plotted the assassination of Archbishop Romero and took part in the 1981 El Mozote massacre of more than 800 men, women, and children.

resonated like thunder throughout Latin America where dozens of activist bishops were being replaced—some hastily defrocked—by pliant champions of conformity. According to the Rev. Joseph Mulligan, an American Jesuit living in Nicaragua, *"these clerics toe the line very carefully on issues of doctrine. They are 'yes-men' doing Rome's bidding."*

Bishop Saenz, a Spanish-born prelate, was a former Vatican liaison to the Salvadoran military and a member of Opus Dei [*god's* work], the extreme right-wing lay organization dedicated to enforcing Catholic dogma. Sáenz eviscerated the *"preferential option for the poor"* of his predecessors, notably Romero, by clamping down on progressive church movements affiliated with Liberation Theology. While cozying up to the ruling party and the plutocrats, Saenz hypocritically defended his stance by arguing that the Roman Catholic Church must speak on behalf of the poor and defenseless ... but never become involved in activism or politics. He then accepted over a million dollars from the country's richest families to resume construction of a cathedral left unfinished by Archbishop Romero who pleaded, *"It is time to build the Church instead of erecting churches."* Much to the Vatican's dismay, Romero had long insisted that it is blasphemy to coddle men's souls while ignoring their earthly needs.

In a plea for *"compassion,"* and in the name of *"national reconciliation"*—a process during which the victims of human rights abuses are urged to forget and their abusers are exonerated—Saenz had asked the Salvadoran government to pardon two former national guardsmen convicted of raping and killing three American nuns, Ita

Ford, Maura Clark, and Dorothy Kazel, and social worker, Jean Donovan in 1980. *"Let us have mercy and pity, for they have demonstrated their repentance,"* Saenz pleaded without a trace of compassion for the women.

Short on political clout but long on memory, the poor in Latin America would not soon forget that John Paul paid a courtesy call on Salvadoran President Armando Calderon Sol, a member of the same political party that engineered Archbishop Romero's assassination, that he cavorted with medal-chested colonels and generals and granted audiences to high-society women sporting low-cut dresses and dripping with diamonds—instead of kneeling at the grave of six slain Jesuit priests. It was during his 1983 visit to Central America that the Pope first clashed with supporters of Liberation Theology. In Managua, he publicly humiliated the Rev. Ernesto Cardenal (1925-2020) a prominent advocate of Liberation Theology who was suspended from the priesthood. The pontiff then *retired* scores of vocal liberal clerics, including the Rev. Bertrand Aristide of Haiti, and Ernesto's brother, the Reverend Fernando Cardenal.

The roots of Liberation Theology are found in the prophetic tradition of evangelists and missionaries in early colonial Latin America—clerics who questioned the Church's elitism and tyrannical power, and who condemned its inhumane treatment of indigenous people and the poor, all converted against their will and forced to renounce their ancestral traditions. Antonio de Montesinos (1480-1540), Bartolomeo de las Casas (1484-1566), and Antonio Vieira (1608-1697) were instrumental in inspiring the social and ecclesiastical dynamism that would later emerge in the pastoral ministry of Liberation Theology.

Hastened by papal nepotism strongly biased in favor of diehard prelates, dilution in the ranks of progressive clergy would be further hastened by martial attitudes that view the faithful as the very enemies of the state. Perceptive and opportunistic, the Church continues to tap into the reactionary power base to maintain both doctrinal monopoly and political custody of the masses. There is a precedent—and a disquieting parallel: Nine hundred years ago the bloodhounds of orthodoxy sniffed heresy. People who held unacceptable views were flung into dungeons. Accused of harboring heretical ideas, forced to confess that they *"transacted with the devil"* (translation: they were freethinkers), that they engaged in heretical pursuits (they hungered for knowledge), and conspired against the established order (they spoke out against corruption and intellectual turpitude), they were tortured with inventive cruelty then killed.

The Church's obscene quest for supremacy, inspired and abetted by successive papal dynasties, was prelude to six Crusades during which thousands of *infidels* were slaughtered. The same *god*-inspired fervor later fanned nearly four centuries of inquisitorial frenzy that devoured Europe and sent another half a million innocent people to the stake while their possessions, confiscated as *evidence*, fattened the Vatican's bulging coffers.

Like Karl Marx, who scorned the proletariat, the Church has never expiated its contempt for the masses, its simulated homophobia, rampant homoeroticism, and flaming misogyny. It steadfastly rejects the notion that people can govern their conscience without its guidance or supervision. Worse, it denies them the right to manage their political destinies by consigning their existence to the same pharisaic elite that their *redeemer* is said to have rebuked.

Few of Christianity's rulers, however pious in appearance, lived up to the principles of the Jewish radical said to have preached compassion, pacifism, and egalitarianism. Faced with a choice between morality and political expediency, Pope John Paul II and his successor, Benedict XVI, opted for the latter. They came to Latin America and told the poor that poverty is good. Then they urged the rich to reject materialism — they might as well have sweet-talked hyenas into giving up a steaming carcass. In Mexico, donning gilded silk vestments, Benedict, who had looked the other way when reports of sexual misconduct by some of his foot soldiers soon exposed a global pattern of priestly pederasty, called for a return to *traditional* Christian values. A day later, in Cuba, he praised democracy then flew back to his sumptuous lodgings in the Vatican, the world's richest and most autarchic empire. In casting out the good shepherds, both popes surrendered the flock to the wolves.

Sic transit gloria mundi.

POPES, PIMPS, PROSTITUTES

A h, the popes. Most Catholics never hear a disparaging word about their *holy fathers,* many of whom have since risen to mythical status. It's as if a perpetual halo of saintliness hovers over their miter-crowned heads. Yet the history of the papacy bears little resemblance with its modern-day portrayal. Over time, the truth about the pontiffs, some of the most savage, warring men ever known, has been obscured. Their true personality and reign were so craftily altered, or glossed over, that few people realize the scale of their profligacy and bloodlust. Egomaniacal, lewd self-promoters who wallowed in vice — traits Catholic historians conceal — popes were widely resented and feared by the laity. When the early glows of the Enlightenment awakened heretofore blinkered minds, freethinkers rebelled against them. Doctrinal disobedience steeled the papacy and led to new pinnacles of barbarism and decadence.

With the unctuous gentility of recent popes as a backdrop, it is hard to imagine that the ancient gurus of Christendom were brutal thugs who retaliated against heresy with unspeakable emotional torments, torture, and death. Popes unleashed, and waded through, torrents of blood to fulfill their earthly objectives and many led their mercenary armies on evangelical fields of battle from which they returned enriched through murder and pillage. In his *Antapodosis,* a florid but highly literate satire, 10th century Bishop Liutbrand of Cremona, Italy, paints a remarkable portrait of the debauchery of the popes — perhaps with a tinge of envy:

> *"They hunted on horses with gold trappings, feasted at rich banquets with dancing girls when the hunt was over, and retired with these shameless whores to beds lined with silk sheets and gold-embroidered covers. All the bishops were married. And their wives made dresses out of the sacred vestments."*

Christian historians dismiss with annoying flippancy the vile character of the most profligate popes, arguing that they never considered them *faultless.* On occasion, the Catholic Encyclopedia provides grudging accounts of papal misconduct. The scandal involving Pope Benedict IX is a case in point. In 1032, after clawing his way to the papacy, he promptly excommunicated clerics he considered hostile and launched a reign of terror. He flung open the doors of the papal palace to sexual deviants and turned it into a lucrative bordello, His violent and licentious conduct infuriated the citizens of Rome, who replaced him with John of Sabine, crowned Sylvester III. But Sylvester was driven out by Benedict's brothers whereupon Benedict sold the papacy to his godfather, Giovanni Graziano, later known as Pope Gregory VI. Benedict then engineered a coup and reclaimed the papal throne. The Church reluctantly remembers him as:

> *"...coarse, immoral, cruel, and indifferent to spiritual things, depraved and unsuited for the ascetic life. He was the worst pope since John XII."*

Or was he?

Fifteenth century Pope Nicholas V issued a papal bull granting the king of Portugal the right to:

"attack, conquer, and subjugate Saracens, pagans and other enemies of Christ, wherever they may be found, to hereditary slavery, and to kill them if necessary."

Pope Urban II granted *"remission of all their sins"* to those *"undertaking a military enterprise designed to liberate eastern churches [those established in Palestine and adjoining areas] from heretics"* — Jews and Muslims.

Aloof, inaccessible, given to fits of hysterical sobbing, utterly inept in statecraft, lacking distinction, and achieving nothing of consequence, Pope Paul II delighted at the sight of naked men being tortured.

Pope Sixtus IV, a champion of the Spanish Inquisition, sired six illegitimate sons, one of them the fruit of an incestuous affair with his own sister.

Innocent VIII instigated severe measures against *"magicians and witches."* He confirmed Tomás de Torquemada as Grand Inquisitor of Spain. He fathered seven illegitimate children. His reign will forever be known as the Golden Age of Bastards.

Pope Julius II obtained the pontificate by fraud and bribery.

Pope Pius II, who fathered [about] twelve illegitimate children, wrote erotic novels. He showered praise on the Prince of Walachia, the notorious Vlad the Impaler who shishkebobed his enemies and fickle friends alike.

Born into the prominent political and banking Florentine Medici family, Pope Leo X was a shopaholic. He financed his spending sprees by selling indulgences, a racket that grants, for a fee, partial or full pardon of earthly sins. He is said to have been engrossed in *"idle and selfish amusements."* Under his pontificate, Christianity assumed a pagan character.

Pope Alexander VI, the notorious Rodrigo Borgia, is without a doubt the most corrupt and evil pontiff in history. He has since become a byword for papal depravity. He finagled his way to St. Peter's by making cardinals out of crooked cronies. He would also appoint his son, Cesare Borgia, and the teenage brother of his mistress cardinals. Being the *holy father* did not prevent Mr. Borgia from indulging in orgies, siring seven children, and engineering the murder of his rivals. To help build alliances. He forced his daughter Lucrezia into three miserable marriages, Her fourth marriage to a man she did not dislike ended in tragedy when the *alliance* went sour and her father ordered to have him stabbed to death. Mr. Borgia encouraged the slave trade in *"conquered lands in the Indies"* to facilitate conversions to Christianity. He died of syphilis.

Pope Paul III created the Congregation of the Holy Office of the Inquisition. His rationale:

> *"Punishment does not take place primarily and per se for the correction and good of the person punished, but for the public good in order that others may become terrified and weaned away from the evils they would commit."*

According to the testimony of Saint Bruno of Cologne, the learned, self-effacing founder of the Carthusian Order of cloistered contemplative monks in 1084:

> *"The whole Church was in wickedness, holiness had faded, justice had perished, and truth had been buried … popes*

and bishops were given to luxury and fornication. The training of the popes left much to be desired, the moral standing of many very low and the practice of celibacy seldom observed. Bishops obtained their offices in irregular ways; their lives and conversations were strangely at variance with their calling. They discharged their duties, not for Christ but for motives of worldly gain. The clergy were in many places regarded with scorn, and their avaricious ideas, opulence, and immorality rapidly gained ground at the center of priestly life. When ecclesiastical authority grew weak at the fountainhead, it necessarily decayed elsewhere. Papal authority lost the respect of many, inspiring resentment against the Curia." {the body of tribunals and offices through which the pope governs].

Expressing contempt for titles, Bruno declined to be made bishop, withdrew with a group of followers and built a monastery in a secluded alpine valley in eastern France.

Saint Peter Damian (1007-1072), an afficionado of self-mortification and the fiercest censor of his age, unrolled a frightful picture of decay in clerical morality in the lurid pages of his Book of Gomorrah, a curious document that remarkably survived centuries of Church cover-ups and book burnings. He wrote:

"A natural tendency to murder and brutalize appears with the popes. Nor do they have any inclination to conquer their abominable lust; many are seen to have employed into licentiousness for an occasion to the flesh, and hence, using this liberty of theirs, perpetuating every crime."

British historian, Lord Acton (1834-1902) summed up the martial nature of the popes when he noted:

> *"They not only murdered in the grand style, but they also
> made murder a legal basis of the Christian Church and a
> condition of salvation."*

Perhaps the popes were dutifully obeying Jesus'
command:

> *"But those mine enemies which would not that I reign over
> them, bring hither and slay* [them] *before me."*
> – Luke (9:27).

◆ ◆ ◆

The *magnificent* 12th and 13th centuries that Christendom
inexplicably glorifies above all others of the Dark Ages
inaugurated the Inquisition, which lingered in various
forms for the next six centuries, and which ushered in the
35-year genocide of the Cathars [also known as the
Albigenses]. The Catholic Encyclopedia readily
acknowledges—and obliquely rationalizes—the Church's
arrogance and tyrannical character when it describes the
Inquisition as the:

> *"...special ecclesiastical institution for combatting or
> suppressing heresy."*

The darker features of that era are not in dispute among
honest historians. In that period of Christian history,
hundreds of thousands of innocent people were
massacred on orders of the Church. In 1182, Pope Lucius
III declared the Cathars heretics and authorized a crusade
against them. Eighty-six years earlier, in 1096, Pope Urban
II approved the first of eight crusades. There would be a
total of nineteen and they went on for 475 years. Heresy,
the Church declared, was a slap in the face of *god*, and it
was the duty of every Christian to kill heretics. Earlier

still, Pope Gregory VII asserted that *"killing heretics is not murder"* and decreed it legal for the Church to slay *"non-believers."* Up until the 19th century, popes forced Christian monarchs to make heresy a crime punishable by death under their civil codes. But it was not heresy that inspired the crusade against the Cathars. Its purpose was to give the papacy additional land and revenues. The popes resorted to unspeakable brutalities to fulfill these objectives.

The Cathars, a peaceful and pious Christian sect who believed that humans are divine souls trapped in a material world created by an imperfect creator, were marked by the Catholic hierarchy for extermination. The crusade against them, a demonstration of the Church's ruthlessness and one of the most gruesome massacres in history began on July 22, 1209, and ended a week later with the death of some 40,000 men, women and children. Shamefully, condemnation of the Church's war against the Cathars, which lasted forty-five years, has been subdued until recent times. Worse, there have been serious attempts to minimize the scope of this infamy and devalue the scale of the carnage to irrelevancy. Such efforts to suppress the truth seem to have bolstered the faith of those who wish to believe, against all reality and common sense, in the saintliness of the Church. The way mainstream Catholic writers make light of this appalling event is unforgivable. The excuse that popes carried out these murders in the name of Christ is indefensible. If we accept the Church's explanation that crusaders were brave men who, imbued with deep religious sentiments, set out to punish those who veered away from orthodox Christianity, then we are accepting the mother of all lies.

What is beyond doubt is that as soon as the Catholic armies were mobilized they became the most formidable killing machine Europe had ever known.

◆◆◆

From the earliest times, religion and politics became intimately intertwined. The cross-fertilization between statecraft and religious objectives has a long and sordid history. Powerful individuals, most often high-ranking members of the clergy, banned essays, pamphlets, and books viewed as anti-religious, particularly those that promote secular humanism (heresy), are deemed seditious (they utter inconvenient truths) or obscene (deeply offensive to feigned standards of decency). These multiple surges of inhibited thought combined to foster a climate of ignorance and intolerance that had a chilling effect on the dissemination and the exchange of rational ideas.

From *The Analects of Confucius* to *Harry Potter and the Sorcerer's Stone*, from Maimonides's *Guide for the Perplexed* to Thomas Paine's *The Age of Reason*, from the *Popol Vuh* and the *Talmud* to *The Adventures of Huckleberry Finn* and *One Flew Over the Cuckoo's Nest*, from Voltaire's *Candide* to Huxley's *Brave New World*, thousands of literary and philosophical masterpieces have been banned, suppressed, and censored to placate the constricted tastes and beliefs of a powerful and vocal minority. Medieval society struggled with arbitrary restrictions enforced by pressure groups prone to subduing the naïve, the unknowing, and the pious with the blackjack tactics of intimidation, intellectual persecution, historical revisionism, and the vilification of individualism.

Widespread in the Middle Ages, the suppression of non-conformist ideas, convincing speculations, and verifiable truths through propaganda, disinformation, and the laundering of impressionable minds survive to this day. If thinking is intrinsic in man, so is—once his mind has been commandeered—his robotic tendency to reject concepts that elude him, defy his version of reality, and undermine his self-view.

◆◆◆

In 1908, The Congregation of the Holy Office of the Inquisition--the Vatican's thought police--is renamed The Sacred Congregation of the Holy Office. In 1965, it is rechristened The Congregation for the Doctrine of the Faith. Cardinal Joseph Alois Ratzinger, the future Pope Benedict XVI, would serve as the prefect of that all-powerful body, whose chief mission is to safeguard and promote Catholic doctrine, faith, and control throughout the world. Under Ratzinger's guidance, the anti-socialist aspect of the Inquisition was beefed up. Two of his acolytes, Cardinals Sebastian Biaggio and Bernardo Gatin (both members of Opus Dei (see next chapter) led a silent campaign that resulted in the defrocking of scores of bishops and parish priests whose greatest sins are to have taught children how to read and write, while encouraging workers to unionize. The new Inquisition's objectives have not changed.

◆◆◆

In January 2009, Pope Benedict XVI, reaching out to the ultra-conservative wing of the Catholic Church, invalidated the excommunication of four schismatic bishops, including one whose denial of the Holocaust provoked outrage. The revocation was seen as a clear sign that Benedict's four-year-old papacy was supporting traditionalists hostile to the sweeping reforms of the Second Vatican Council, which sought to create a more modern and open Church. Among the men reinstated was Bishop Richard Williamson, a British-born cleric who, a week earlier, had told an interviewer:

"I believe that the historical evidence is hugely against six million [Jews] having been deliberately gassed in gas chambers as a deliberate policy of Adolf Hitler. I believe there were no gas chambers."

Williamson was elaborating on a speech he had delivered twenty years earlier at Notre-Dame-de Lourdes church in Sherbrooke, Québec, Canada:

"There was not a single Jew killed in the gas chamber. It was all lies, lies, lies. The Jews created the Holocaust so we would prostrate ourselves on our knees before them and approve of their new State of Israel... Protestants get their orders from the devil and the Vatican has sold it soul to liberalism."

Like Williamson, the other reinstated men were members of the Society of St. Pius X, founded by extreme right-wing French Archbishop Marcel Lefebvre (1905-1991) in 1970 to protest the modernizing reforms of Vatican II. Lefebvre made the men bishops in unsanctioned consecrations, prompting his immediate excommunication and that of the other men by John Paul II.

Somehow, traditions that inhibit religious freedom and promote antisemitism do not enhance Church unity or improve its reputation. But Pope Benedict XVI would eventually make other concessions to Lefebvre's followers. He allowed a broader recitation of the Tridentine rite, a service that includes a prayer for the mass conversion of Jews.

◆◆◆

Pope Benedict visited Israel in May 2009. Visibly ill at ease, a diffident smile on his lips and the oblique, furtive gaze of a coward or hypocrite faking humility, the pontiff spoke like a scholar, like someone observing a not-so-distant past from the secure sidelines of officialdom. It is clear that the horrors to which he alluded with studied aloofness had little more than academic significance. He failed to mention the Nazis by name, to characterize their actions as cold-blooded murder. He glossed over his own past so he wouldn't have to explain it. A papal spokesman laconically defended Benedict:

"He can't mention everything every time he speaks."

While Benedict's past as a member of the Hitler youth and a solider in the German army was widely acknowledged, it was understandably very difficult for some people to go past it. What revolted me — I lost nine-tenths of my family to Hitler's gas chambers--is that *princes of the Church*, meeting in secret conclave in the Sistine Chapel, knowing these facts and aware of the Church's unabashed sympathy for the Nazis, chose among all the candidates for the papacy, some from Third World nations, to elect the man who would call himself Benedict [blessed]. This was willful blindness or arrogance or both. Certainly, they knew their choice would unsettle at least one group of people sharing a long and difficult history with the Church. Certainly, they might have foreseen a moment when the pope would stand before a Holocaust memorial and be seen as a representative of both his Church and his antecedents. Yet, they went ahead, as if by design, and appointed as the head of an empire with the Vatican's infamous record a man with an equally discreditable history. Benedict could have easily addressed those issues in the nation whose very creation was in part the product of that abomination. The Vatican's vacuous argument that he had addressed them before was unconvincing because by choosing not to do so in the one place where such a statement of acknowledgement and regret would have made the most difference, he raised questions not about a choice but, no doubt commanded by *god*, the motive behind it.

OPUS DEI'S STRANGE BEDFELLOWS

Outside its own doctrinaire circle of followers and fans, Opus Dei, or *god's* work, has a dappled reputation, mostly bad, Andrew Greeley (1928-2013), the eminent American Catholic priest, sociologist, journalist, and best-selling author, described it as,

> *"a devious, antidemocratic, reactionary, semi-fascist institution desperately famished for absolute dominion in the* [Catholic] *Church and quite possibly very close now to having that power."*

Labelling the elite group, *"authoritarian and power mad,"* Greeley warned that,

> *"Opus Dei is an extremely dangerous organization because it appeals to the love of secrecy and the power lust of certain kinds of religious personalities. It may well be the most powerful group in the Church today. It is capable of doing an enormous amount of harm. It ought to be forced out of the shadows or suppressed."*

Opus Dei has about 200,000 members worldwide. Some 3,000 are priests. Armed with this international cohort of dedicated warriors, Opus Dei has successfully penetrated schools and universities, banks, publishing houses, television and radio networks, movie companies, ad agencies, and even the U.S. Supreme Court: Justices Amy Coney Barrett, John Roberts, Clarence Thomas, Brett Kavanaugh, and Samuel Alito are said to either belong to or support Opus Dei's objectives.* The organization has been accused of deceptive and aggressive recruitment practices, including *"love bombing,"* – the syrupy show of affection used to lure, conscript, and convert members.

The core mission of Opus Dei, in the words of the British daily, *The Guardian,* is *"to help shape the world in a Catholic manner."* Helpers include clergy, captains of industry, the military, and government officials. The super-stealthy organization was founded just before the Spanish Civil War and blossomed in the halcyon Catholic days of El Caudillo, fascist dictator Francisco Franco's crusade against the Republican left. When Opus Dei came to prominence in the late 1960s it was because Franco's cabinet included an inordinate number of *Opusdeistas* – too many to be the result of coincidence.

Opus Dei, which strives for a reunification of church and state, arms its members with special and far-reaching powers driven by the *divinely inspired* longing to cleanse the world of *"heretics and deliver wicked, rudderless humanity, by force, if necessary into Christ's loving arms."* The 900-year-old organization was formerly known as the Sovereign Military Hospitaller Order of the Saints John of Jerusalem, Rhodes and Malta. Modeled after an ancient group of soldier-monks who massacred infidels (Jews, Muslims, Cathars) Knights of Malta ceremonies and

---

* The devout Catholic and ultraconservative Amy Coney Barrett, a fierce defender of the Second Amendment who dissented when a court upheld a federal law prohibiting felons from possessing firearms, is best remembered for joining the other five justices in sanctioning, in defiance of the 6th commandment, the execution of an African American felon.

rituals *"inculcate lessons of chivalry and courage and inspire a militant spirit in opposition to all non-Christian ideologies and powers."* The Knights are influential Vatican surrogates with extensive ties to right-wing intelligence networks.[*]

Originally trained as death squads during the Crusades, later adopting a fiercely anti-*communist* stance, the Knights were instrumental in the creation of the Central Intelligence Agency. They also took part in U.S. global *black* (covert) operations. The founding fathers of the Office of Strategic Services (OSS), the precursor to the CIA, William "Wild Bill" Donovan (1883-1959) and Allen Dulles, (1893-1969) the longest-serving CIA director, were Knights, as were many in the CIA hierarchy, including John F. Kennedy's director, John McCone (1902-1991), who helped engineer the 1973 military coup against Chile's democratically elected president, Salvador Allende; and Ronald Reagan's director, William Casey (1913-1987).who would be accused of involvement with the controversial Iran-Contra affair, in which the Reagan administration secretly traded arms to the Islamic Republic of Iran, and diverted some of the resulting income to aid the rebel Contras in Nicaragua.

There is compelling evidence that the Knights of Malta were linked to the *"Rat Run,"* the post-World War II getaway route used by Nazi top brass and death camp

[*] In 2022 Pope Francis dissolved the leadership of the Knights of Malta and installed a provisional government ahead of the election of a new Grand Master. The change came after five years of often acrimonious debate within the order and between some top members of the old guard and the Vatican over a new constitution that some feared would weaken its sovereignty.

"scientists" to escape to the Americas. These thugs were issued new identities and special credentials that protected them from prosecution for crimes against humanity. One of them, Major General Reinhard Gehlen (1902-1979), a devout Catholic and legendary Cold War spymaster, surrendered to the U.S. Army Counter-Intelligence Corps in 1945. Flown to Washington, Gehlen went to work for Donovan and Dulles. Overcome with gratitude, Gehlen handed over the names of several OSS officers suspected of being *communist* sympathizers. Gehlen employed hundreds of "ex-Nazis," among them Alois Brunner, Adolf Eichman's right-hand man. Brunner was responsible for the slaughter of 140,000 Austrian, Greek, French, and Slovak Jews. The CIA turned a blind eye and given the exigencies of the Cold War, even took part in some of Gehlen's operations.

In appreciation for his work, Gehlen, Hitler's Eastern Front intelligence chief who organized and took part in atrocities against Jews, Roma, and Slavs, was awarded the Knights of Malta's highest decoration, the Grand Cross of Merit for his *"devotion to Christian principles"*

Writing in *The People of god*, American journalist, Penny Lernoux (1940-1989) stated that:

> *"After World War II, the Vatican, the OSS, elements of the SS, and various branches of the Sovereign Military Order of Malta joined ... to help Nazi war criminals escape."*

Documents reveal that New York Cardinal Francis Spellman (1889-1967), head of the Knights in the U.S., was implicated in the 1954 right-wing military coup in Guatemala, a country that, along with Honduras, I would get to know during my 12-year (1994-2006) assignments in Central America where 200,000 indigenous people were murdered and disappeared, a genocide in which the CIA has acknowledged complicity. Spellman was also linked to organized crime by his long association with Archbishop Paul Marcinkus (1922-2006), the former head of the Vatican Bank and a suspect in the shady death of Pope John Paul I a month after his coronation.

One of the Knights of Malta's main spheres of influence was Latin America, where fascists and escaped Nazis were welcomed with all the trappings of Christian charity. Chilean strongman, General Augusto Pinochet (1915-2006), a CIA stooge and convicted human rights violator who introduced the Death Flights, extrajudicial killings in which victims were dropped to their death from airplanes and helicopters into oceans, rivers, and even mountains ... was a devout Knight. So was *"Our man in Lima,"* deposed Peruvian dictator, Alberto Fujimori, recently released from a 24-year prison sentence for embezzlement and human rights abuses. So was the charismatic Argentinian president, General Juan Perón (1895-1974) who, declassified CIA documents reveal, laundered Nazi gold through the Vatican Bank, and is widely believed to have channeled covert U.S. funds to Poland's Solidarity trade union and transferred laundered money from the illegal sale of arms to the Contras through the Vatican Bank, the main shareholder of the Italian scandal-ridden Banco Ambrosiano.

◆ ◆ ◆

Dubbed the "American Nietzsche," H. L Mencken (1880-1956) defined religion as *"the illogical belief in the occurrence of the improbable."* With characteristic ferocity, Nietzsche viewed it as belief system that reduces the faithful *"to not wanting to know what is true. It's an affair of the rabble."* While conceding its tenuous potential as a source for good, I see religion as a supercilious, divisive, and exclusionary artifice engineered to keep people emotionally enslaved, ignorant, and stupid. Like capitalism, which it tacitly endorses, religion is a diseased and avaricious system driven by and dedicated to the fattening of the corporate queen at the expense of captive worker ants. Like capitalism, it is fickle and blind to human suffering. The deep and palpable despair felt by Latin America's poor, whose faith in the hereafter exceeds their prospects in the here and now, can be characterized as a rational response to an inescapable kismet that religion cannot forestall. For them, such predestination includes more of the same.

◆◆◆

In Guatemala, when morgue records don't add up, it's collusion, not lousy accounting. The news was bad enough. That year had witnessed the highest official number of extrajudicial executions of street children—thirteen in all. Some had been tortured, others had been summarily shot to death for pilfering food or stealing trifles that might have bought them their next meal.

Surely thirteen homeless minors murdered in cold blood is thirteen too many. But were there more? Unaccounted for? Forgotten? Hurriedly dispatched through the bureaucratic maze, then nullified, voided as if they had never been born? Sometimes, when numbers make no sense, when facts are treated as fiction and no one will explain the discrepancies, one must inventory the bodies and reconstruct the truth.

What I discovered in the forensic records of Guatemala City's Judiciary Morgue suggests more than just bad arithmetic. It reeked of complicity to alter documents, all part of a deliberate scheme to soft-pedal or conceal an unrelenting spree of sponsored assassinations. My findings revealed that:

♦ Of the two hundred and thirty-four kids aged 9 to 17 who had died in one year, 114 died of *"massive gunshot wounds to the head, chest and/or abdomen."* However succinct, descriptions of the trauma they endured unequivocally suggest that the weapons had been fired at or near point-blank range.

♦ Seventy-six died from causes less well defined or ambiguously described as *"brain trauma," "cerebral hemorrhage," "cranial contusions,"* and *"cervical fractures."* In several cases, the cause of death was laconically labelled *"indeterminate"* or *"unavailable."*

♦ Fifteen were registered XX—*"unknown"* in the lingo of indifference. Among them were seven kids whose identity was widely known, two of them 14-year-old boys who were found face down in a garbage-strewn ditch—both had been shot through the head—and an 11-year-old boy who died from massive injuries sustained when an explosive device placed in a fast-food container blew up in his face.

♦ Nine were said to have drowned, an improbable scenario unless they were pushed head-first into the water and held submerged in one of the city's members-only swimming pools.

I shared my findings with a forensic pathologist, a morgue attendant, an emergency room physician, and a pediatrician. All declined comment. Met in private and guaranteed anonymity, the retired legal adviser to a children's advocacy group cautiously suggested that *"overwork and ineptitude, rather than corruption are at the root of this bad, if alarming, accounting."* He then acknowledged that misinformation is often used as a disinformation tool because *"it is more expedient to lie than audit for errors."* Pressed on, he squarely put the blame on the courts, *"which have been handed the power to determine the cause of death based on legal loopholes rather than sound medicine."* With a reluctance born of embarrassment (or justifiable fear), he painted a picture of chaos, incompetence, finger-pointing, and inertia within Guatemala's judicial system.

Indeed. Lacking an effective criminal justice system, Guatemalans are prone to take the law into their own hands. Street children are viewed as *"vermin,"* and *"bad for the nation's image and reputation."* Somehow, no one takes issue with the entrenched and deplorable economic and socio-political realities that spawn such a large number of homeless minors. There is no justice in Guatemala (or for that matter in Honduras, Nicaragua, and El Salvador). Children are abandoned by their overly procreative parents, persecuted by the state, ignored by the Church, and rejected by society.

◆◆◆

Eyewitnesses and gruesome photographs obtained by this writer confirm that homeless minors have been routinely abducted, beaten, burned with cigarettes, subjected to mock executions, and sexually assaulted by police and private security guards. Some had their ears torn off (they had overheard damning chatter). Others had their tongues ripped out (they had snitched). Several had their eyes gouged (they had witnessed criminal activity by agents of the state) before the merciful coup de grace, generally a blow to the head or a bullet to the base of the neck put an end to their ordeal. Most were pushed into the ravines that gird the city's shantytowns, stinking chasms littered with garbage and human waste, and patrolled by feral dogs, vultures, and desperados. I carried out many of my investigations strapped in a lightweight bulletproof vest aimed at shielding me not against crime lords or common thugs but against soldiers and cops.

"We've seen human rights take a back seat to trade and diplomatic concerns," grieved an Amnesty International spokesperson. Violations continue to defile a region hopelessly crippled by wars and disfigured by hunger and disease.

In Central America, an area historically traumatized by political and social turmoil, crippled by wild swings from dictatorship to anarchy to inept, apathetic civilian puppet regimes and back, human rights violations are legion. And in Guatemala, the Land of Eternal Spring, a country kneaded by cataclysmic volcanic and seismic events, crimes against humanity often eclipse its deceptive beauty.

Annoyance rather than outrage at Guatemala's apathy and unwillingness to address what had begun to draw scrutiny, prompted the U.S. — Guatemala's economic and military godfather—to suspend weapons deliveries. Expressing *"grave concern"* over what he termed *"an escalating spree of state-sponsored disappearances and extrajudicial executions,"* Congressman Jim McDermott (D.-Washington) one of a two-member congressional fact-finding team, told this writer that U.S. foreign policy in Central America had been *"an unending disaster. We have a history of picking the wrong sides, of aiding and abetting despotic regimes. Adding insult to injury, the U.S. is the only western nation that refuses to sign and ratify the United Nations Children's Right Convention."*

◆◆◆

Titled *The Mathematics of Death* and published under my byline in three Central American mainstream dailies, the exposé earned me the first of two death threats. Hoping for an attentive ear from two of America's foremost *spiritual* leaders and urging them to submit a short statement in support of the children, I sent copies of the article to Billy Graham and New York's John Cardinal O'Connor. They responded as follows:

"The Reverend Billy Graham is too busy to comment on this issue." The letter was signed, The Billy Graham Evangelical Association. Not to be outdone, *"His Eminence has asked me to inform you that he has no time to comment on the issues addressed in your article."* – Father Whalen, spokesman for John Cardinal O'Connor.

This callous indifference was replayed when Guatemala's First and Second Ladies, both touted as ardent supporters of children's rights, both bluebloods and devout Catholics, failed to show up at a pre-arranged interview with this writer. No apology or explanation was ever issued. I shrugged off this affront to the bad manners of the self-important and to their lack of respect for other people's time, a trait characteristic among people of the region. Ironically, it is those most apt to help cleanse *"the sins that cry to heaven for vengeance"* — oppression of the poor and voiceless — whose hearts turn to stone.

SCOURGE THE FLESH, SAVE THE SOUL

A round 430 BC, not long after a war between Athens and Sparta set the Peloponnese on fire, an epidemic ravaged the people of Athens. It lasted five years. Some estimates put the death toll at 100,000. The Greek historian Thucydides (460-400 BC) wrote that:

> *"People in good health were all of a sudden attacked by violent heats in the head, and redness and inflammation in the eyes, the inward parts, such as the throat or tongue, becoming bloody and emitting an unnatural and fetid breath."*

What exactly this epidemic proved to be has long been a source of debate among scientists. A number of diseases have been put forward as possibilities, including typhoid fever and Ebola. Many scholars believe that overcrowding caused by the war exacerbated the epidemic.

The Black Death traveled from Asia to Europe, leaving devastation in its wake. Some estimates suggest that it wiped out over half of Europe's population. It was caused by a strain of the bacterium *Yersinia pestis* which is likely extinct today and was spread by flea-infested rodents. The bodies of victims were buried in mass graves.

The infection that caused the Cocoliztli epidemic was a form of viral hemorrhagic fever that killed 15 million inhabitants of Mexico and Central America. Among a population already weakened by extreme drought, the disease proved to be catastrophic. "Cocoliztli" is the Aztec word for "pest." A recent study that examined DNA from the skeletons of victims found that they were infected with a subspecies of Salmonella known as *S. para typhi C*, which causes enteric fever, a category of fevers that includes typhoid. Enteric fever can cause dehydration and gastrointestinal problems. It is still a major health threat today.

The so-called American Plagues were a cluster of Eurasian diseases brought to the Americas by European explorers. These illnesses, including smallpox, contributed to the collapse of the Aztec, Mayan, and Inca civilizations. These diseases helped a Spanish force, led by Hernán Cortés, to conquer the Aztec capital of Tenochtitlán in 1519. Another Spanish force led by Francisco Pizarro conquered the Incas in 1532. The Spanish took over the territories of both empires. In both cases, the Aztec and Incan armies had been ravaged by disease and were unable to withstand the Spanish onslaught.

When people from Britain, France, Portugal, and the Netherlands began exploring, conquering and settling the Americas, they were helped by the fact that disease had vastly reduced the size of any indigenous groups that opposed them.

The Black Death's last major outbreak in Great Britain caused a mass exodus from London, led by King Charles II. The plague started in April 1665 and spread rapidly through the hot summer months. Fleas from plague-infected rodents were one of the main causes of transmission. By the time the plague ended, about 100,000 people, including 15% of London's population, had died.

The 1720 Great Bubonic Plague of Marseille erupted

when the three-masted *Grand-Saint-Antoine,* docked in Marseille, France, carrying a cargo of goods from the eastern Mediterranean. Although the ship was quarantined, plague seeped into the city, likely through fleas on plague-infected rodents. The plague spread quickly and, over the next three years, as many as 100,000 people died in Marseille and adjoining areas of Provence. It's estimated that up to 30% of the population of Marseille may have perished.

Fifty years later, in plague-ravaged Moscow, the terror of quarantined citizens erupted into violence. Riots spread through the city and culminated in the murder of Archbishop Ambrosius, who encouraged crowds not to gather for worship. The empress of Russia, Catherine II (1729-1796), was so desperate to contain the plague and restore public order that she issued a hasty decree ordering all factories to be moved out of Moscow. By the time the plague ended, as many as 100,000 people may have died. Even after the plague subsided, Catherine struggled to restore order. In 1773, Yemelyan Pugachev, a man who claimed to be Peter III (Catherine's executed husband), led an insurrection that resulted in the deaths of thousands more.

When yellow fever erupted in Philadelphia in 1793, officials wrongly believed that slaves were immune. As a result, abolitionists called for people of African origin to be recruited to nurse the sick. The disease is carried and transmitted by mosquitoes, which experienced a population boom during the particularly hot and humid summer weather that year. It wasn't until winter arrived—and the mosquitoes died out—that the epidemic fizzled out. By then, more than 5,000 people had perished.

In the modern industrial age, new transport links made it easier for influenza viruses to wreak havoc. In just a few months, the disease spanned the globe, killing one million people. It took just five weeks for the epidemic to reach peak mortality. The earliest cases were reported in Russia. The virus spread rapidly in St. Petersburg before it made its way through Europe and, despite the fact that air travel didn't exist yet, the rest of the world,

A polio epidemic that started in New York City caused 27,000 cases and 6,000 deaths in the U.S. The disease mainly affects children and sometimes leaves survivors with permanent disabilities. Polio epidemics occurred sporadically in the U.S. until the Salk vaccine was developed in 1954. As the vaccine became widely available, cases declined. The last polio case in the U.S. was reported in 1979. Worldwide vaccination efforts have greatly reduced the disease, although it has not yet been completely eradicated.

An estimated 500 million people from the South Seas to the North Pole fell victim to the Spanish Flu. One-fifth died, with some indigenous communities pushed to the brink of extinction. The flu's spread and lethality were enhanced by the cramped conditions of soldiers and poor wartime nutrition that many people were experiencing during World War I. Despite its name, the disease likely did not originate in Spain. Spain was a neutral nation during the war and did not enforce strict censorship of its press, which could therefore freely publish early accounts of the illness. As a result, people falsely believed the illness was specific to Spain, and the name Spanish Flu stuck.

The 1957-58 Asian Flu pandemic was another global showing for influenza. With its roots in China, the disease claimed more than one million lives. The virus that caused the pandemic was a blend of avian flu viruses. The Centers for Disease Control and Prevention (CDC) notes that the disease spread rapidly and was reported in Singapore in February 1957, Hong Kong in April 1957, and the coastal cities of the U.S. in the summer of 1957. The total death toll was more than 1.1 million worldwide, with 116,000 deaths occurring in the U.S.

AIDS has claimed an estimated 35 million lives since it was first identified in 1981. HIV, the virus that causes AIDS, likely developed from a chimpanzee virus that transferred to humans in West Africa in the 1920s. The virus made its way around the world, and the disease bloomed into a pandemic by the late 20th century. About 64% of the estimated 40 million now afflicted with the human immunodeficiency virus live in sub-Saharan Africa. For decades, the disease had no known cure, but medications developed in the 1990s now allow people with the disease to live a normal life span with regular treatment.

The 2009 swine flu pandemic was caused by a new strain of H1N1 that originated in Mexico in the spring of 2009 before spreading to the rest of the world. In one year, according to the CDC, the virus infected as many as 1.4 billion people across the globe and killed upwards of 400,000 people. The 2009 flu pandemic primarily affected children and young adults, and 80% of the deaths were in people younger than 65. That was unusual, considering that most strains of flu viruses, including those that cause seasonal flu, cause the highest percentage of deaths in people ages 65 and older.

Ebola ravaged West Africa between 2014 and 2016, with 28,600 reported cases and 11,325 deaths. The first case to be reported was in Guinea in December 2013, then the disease quickly spread to Liberia and Sierra Leone. The bulk of the cases and deaths occurred in those three countries. A smaller number of cases occurred in Nigeria, Mali, Senegal, the U.S., and parts of Europe. There is no cure for Ebola, although efforts at finding a vaccine continue. The first known cases of Ebola occurred in Sudan and the Democratic Republic of Congo in 1976, and the virus may have originated in bats.

The impact of the recent Zika epidemic in South America and Central America won't be known for several years. In the meantime, scientists face a race against time to bring the virus under control. The Zika virus is usually spread through mosquitoes of the Aedes genus, although it can also be sexually transmitted in humans. While Zika is usually not harmful to adults or children, it can attack fetuses and cause birth defects. The type of mosquitoes that carry Zika flourish best in warm, humid climates, making South and Central America, and parts of the southern U.S. prime areas for the virus to flourish.

The ongoing COVID-19 pandemic, driven by the novel coronavirus SARS-CoV-2, may be the world's deadliest viral outbreak in more than a century. From the virus' initial detection in December 2019 to mid-December 2020, the pathogen infected at least 75 million people and caused

1.6 million deaths. As of September. 2021, COVID-19 had killed more people in the U.S. than the so-called Spanish flu did during the 1918 pandemic. That said, in total, the 1918 pandemic claimed more than 50 million lives worldwide, out of a global population of roughly 1.8 billion people; the death toll was high, in part, because no vaccines were available at the time and doctors lacked antibiotics to treat secondary bacterial infections. By comparison, today's global population is nearly 8 billion, and as of mid-August 2022, about 6.4 million people had died of COVID-19, although the reported number of confirmed deaths is likely lower than the true total. At this writing, there were 769,806,130 global confirmed cases and 6,955,497 deaths.

Though it had been around for ages, leprosy grew into a pandemic in Europe in the Middle Ages, resulting in the building of numerous leprosy-focused hospitals to accommodate the vast number of victims. A slow-developing bacterial disease that causes sores and deformities, leprosy was believed to be a punishment from *god* that ran in families. This belief led to moral judgments and ostracization of victims. Now known as Hansen's disease, it still afflicts tens of thousands of people a year and can be fatal if not treated with antibiotics. Leprosy is an age-old disease and is described in the literature of ancient civilizations. It is a chronic infectious disease which is caused by a type of bacterium called Mycobacterium leprae. The disease affects the skin, the peripheral nerves, mucosa of the upper respiratory tract, and the eyes. Leprosy is curable and treatment in the early stages can prevent disability. Apart from physical deformities, persons affected by leprosy also face stigmatization and discrimination. According to World Health Organization (WHO), leprosy is a neglected tropical disease which still occurs in more than 120 countries, with more than 200,000 new cases reported every year. Eradication of leprosy as a public health problem globally (defined as prevalence of less than 1 per 10,000 population) was achieved in 2000 and in most countries by 2010. The reduction in the number of new cases has been gradual. As per data of 2019, Brazil, India and Indonesia reported more than 10,000 new cases, while thirteen other countries (Bangladesh, Democratic Republic of the Congo, Ethiopia, Madagascar, Mozambique, Myanmar, Nepal, Nigeria, Philippines, Somalia, South Sudan, Sri Lanka and the United Republic of Tanzania) each reported between 1,000–10,000 new cases. About 200,000 new cases of leprosy are reported every year.

Syphilis is a sexually transmitted disease generally believed to have originated from the New World, imported into Europe by Christopher Columbus's sailors and missionaries after their famous voyages to the "Indies.". The first recorded outbreak of syphilis in Europe occurred in 1494/1495 in Naples, Italy, during a French invasion. Because it was spread by returning French troops, the ailment was known as "French disease." It was not until 1530 that the term "syphilis" was first coined by the Italian physician and poet Girolamo Fracastoro. The causative organism, *Treponema pallidum,* was first identified by Fritz Schaudinn and Erich Hoffmann in 1905 at the Charité Clinic in Berlin. The first effective treatment, Salvarsan, was developed in 1910 by prominent Japanese bacteriologist, Sahachiro Hata. It was followed by the introduction of penicillin in 1943. In 2020, WHO estimated that 7.1 million adults aged 15–49 acquired syphilis globally. Some countries that monitor syphilis are showing a troubling increase in syphilis cases among men who have sex with men, including congenital syphilis. In 2016 (the latest available estimate), seven in every 1,000 pregnant women had syphilis Left untreated, syphilis can lead to blindness, neurological problems, insanity, and death.

During the Dark Ages, a period marked by intellectual and cultural decline, many of the above scourges were blamed on Jews.

◆◆◆

It was soon after my father's death—I was 50, he was 83— intrigued by his stormy recantations and anxious to reaffirm some of my own instinctive preconceptions, that I ventured, for the first time, in the Kabbalah's arcane realm. Enthralled and bewildered at first, often driven to mental exhaustion, I eventually tired of its multilayered circularity, glaring contradictions, and maddening esotericism. I found such mental pirouettes more taxing than I'd imagined. Faced with its imponderable assertions and rigid demands, I bowed out, stunned by its bewildering ruses, its ability to disconcert by elevating paradox to astral heights. All in all, my brief foray into Jewish mysticism was not in vain. Careful, measured readings yielded fresh insights on the magnitude of Jewish thought. I would later recognize the influence it would have on the works of Pico Della Mirandola, Benedict (Baruch) Spinoza, Gottfried Leibniz, Emmanuel Swedenborg, Franz Kafka,, Jorge Luis Borges, Walter

Benjamin, and Jacque Derrida. I would also speculate that the roots of the Kabbalistic doctrines had been enunciated much earlier than traditional practitioners insist—that they predate world religions, forming the primordial blueprint for Creation's philosophies, religions, sciences, arts, and political systems, whereas historically, Kabbalah emerged from earlier forms of Jewish mysticism, in 12th- to 13th-century Spain and southern France—that it had tapped, in considerably simpler language and form into the Tao and other Buddhist teachings. No matter the originality of a concept, *"There is nothing new under the sun"* (Ecclesiastes, 1:9) I must believe that I was transformed, however imperceptibly, by the Kabbalah's cerebral exactions and mesmerizing nonsense.

◆ ◆ ◆

Once imparted and seized, ideas—the sublime and the ridiculous—take a life of their own. The ridiculous ones cannot easily be jettisoned. Witness the assertion of a man who demonstrated *god*'s existence by insisting, "I believe in *god, therefore* he exists!"

PASTOR MIKE,
OR THE TRIUMPH OF HYPOCRISY

The true hypocrite, wrote French novelist André Gide (1869-1951) *"is the one who ceases to perceive his deception, the one who lies with sincerity."* One of the weapons dream-busters wield to promote their own vision of reality is deception. The quarrels that cleave society stem from the frenzied tug-of-war between conflicting ideas. Essential truths are trampled in the process. Everyone has beliefs, convictions, worldviews. Many of our perceptions are erected on a vast scaffolding of dogmas—usually someone else's. Keen on cramming dormant brain cells, we adopt these fictions from childhood. We fiercely cling to them, falsely claiming that they are the offspring of our own cogitations because they encourage us not to think, because they shield us from what we fear most—the bewildering ambiguities of perceived reality—because they keep us warm and cozy in our self-spun ideological cocoons.

I face my reality and bare my dreams in everything I do, say, and write, mindful that candor is unnerving (but savoring its improprieties), aware that the truth will trigger caustic ripostes and bitter denunciations (and exulting in their advent). A critique of organized religion I published in a mainstream daily some time ago elicited several ad hominem attacks, which I anticipated and disregarded. Much to my amazement, it also inspired a letter to the editor, sensitive and engaging, revealing the ostensible maturity and refinement of its author. It was a peace offering I could not in good conscience ignore.

Mike Gaston, now ex-pastor at the Grace Baptist Church in Santa Clarita, California, invited me to attend a service, "no strings attached," he added. I have no religion, but I'm blessed with enough mental elasticity to know that we live in a world of memories and imprinted beliefs that sometimes obscure our horizons, and that useful insights can be gleaned in the strangest of places. Unlike zealots, rational individuals go beyond what they have been habituated to accept at face value. I was certain, digesting Pastor Mike's engaging letter, that I had nothing to lose by accepting his invitation. I drove the forty-odd miles to witness the awesome and stirring spectacle of an Evangelical Easter Sunday celebration.

Grace Baptist Church is a gargantuan house of worship reminiscent of New York's Radio City Music Hall. It boasts a gallery worthy of the Paris Opera House and a two-tier stage on which perform a star-quality orchestra and an all-congregant choir. There wasn't an empty seat. The mood was alternately contemplative and upbeat. I knew I was in the presence of a phenomenal happening, but I glimpsed no burning bush, experienced no epiphany. I did not faint in a state of ecstatic rapture or begin to speak in tongues. I was attending a superbly well staged production, part show business, part hard proselytism, part contagious histrionics.

Pastor Mike is an emotive and skillful revivalist. He relies on ad-libbed inspiration, not a script. He speaks from the heart, with an enthusiasm born of conviction and driven by seemingly limitless energy. He conveys, without theatricality, a vivid sense of his reality of *god*. Abstaining from the hysterics and hyperboles common among televangelists, he speaks with fervor, not fanaticism. His method is his faith. I saw in him a profoundly human individual, open-minded and strangely tolerant of heterodox ideas, and endowed with an infectious sense of humor.

Meeting Pastor Mike and breaking bread with him as we did after the services at his favorite restaurant, was an event that I celebrated both on a cosmic and personal level. It is always gratifying to extend a hand across the great divide of dissimilar persuasions and, in the process, to cultivate a newfound acquaintance. Pastor Mike must have sensed that I would never get *religion*. The fact that he appeared to accept me as I am (or am not) suggested, I thought, that I was in the presence of a kindly, forbearing man. Was this the onset of a budding, dogma-free, amity?

We are not all hewn from the same ashlars. While I continue to view religion as a wall-building con, I recognize that exceptionally large numbers of people seek and find comfort in its bosom. Faith makes the obvious tolerable (or irrelevant). Conviction and wishful thinking surpass our ability to challenge the absurdities that only unflinching faith makes real. I make do with what I know, what I can see, hear, and touch. When one cannot seek solace in make-believe, one must trust reason.

In his homily, Pastor Mike cautioned the congregation against using the word "watershed" too freely, as it should reflect only significant milestones in our lives. I have never used the term, lightly or otherwise. Yet, what transpired a year or so later can only be characterized as a turning point, a crisis, a defining moment that deepened my distrust of those who claim to speak for *god*. Any truth

that owes its existence to blind, raging faith, I was forced
to conclude, must be a lie. The olive branch Pastor Mike
had extended—a clever proselytizing stunt, I would soon
discover—turned out to be a barbed whip that scourged
my hide raw and wounded my soul. Sadly, it would also
remind me of how bad a judge of character I can be, how I
tend to let my guard down when courted by smiling
charlatans.

◆ ◆ ◆

My older son, unbeknownst to me, had embraced
Messianic Judaism, the most virulent and sinister
Christian Evangelical cult dedicated to converting Jews to
Christianity by promoting the false, preposterous, and
offensive notion that Jews can accept Jesus as their
messiah and still be Jewish. I was heartbroken. I saw in
this startling defection a callous disavowal of his parents,
a repudiation of his extended family, and, worse, a
desertion from his tribe. Wearing a star of David and
insisting that he is now a "better Jew than ever," he is
doctrinally and unabashedly a Christian who deviously
refers to himself as a Jew, but the basis of his theology is
that Jesus was the messiah and that he died for the sins of
mankind. There is in this assertion a visceral, if
subconscious, hint of anti-Jewishness that Jesus himself--
had he been accurately quoted by contemporaries instead
of "according to" agenda-driven disciples more than fifty
years after his death--would have repudiated.

Guarded in the beginning, my son's disclosure did not
end there. He proceeded to blitz me with quotations from
Scriptures (almost exclusively from the New Testament).
When I protested, he pressured me to accept Jesus lest I

incur the fires of hell. Nothing in his upbringing—progressive and secular—hinted at such bizarre metamorphosis. Had he somehow been brainwashed or was he courting lunacy? I couldn't tell. Distraught, in need of counsel, seeking answers, craving for an attentive ear, perhaps a caring heart, and in hopes of comprehending the causes and dynamics of apostasy, I turned to Pastor Mike.

Pastor Mike greeted the news with controlled jubilation. But when I expressed bitterness and grief, his ear turned inattentive, his heart hardened to stone and his mouth oozed the zealotry, the furious pomposity, and the transparent antisemitism of a Christian crusader. Instead of empathizing, finding words of consolation, or venturing a rationale, even bland, for my son's transfiguration, he screamed.

"You are the apostate, the absconder, the heretic, the Judas. You and your kind are the reason why Jews—the unperfected Christians—can never be saved. Only Jesus can bring redemption to your cursed race." *Unperfected?*

I kept my cool and quoted the Fifth Commandment. "Is this how a son honors his father, threatening him, wishing upon him the horrors of Hades?"

"Your son is right," Pastor Mike shrieked. "He found the truth. He now lives it. Follow him or you are doomed." I thanked Pastor Mike for his solicitude and hung up. So much for the fiction of good will among men. So much for Christian charity. When love for *god* is so great that it allows hatred to infect it, evil is at work, not love.

Dazed, I confided in Rabbi Yehuda Lazar at the nearby Chabad Center, a small, unassuming prayer hall tucked away in a corner of a modest strip mall. I wept. Rabbi Lazar, a self-effacing, soft-spoken man, looked at me intently for a while, a hint of sadness arching his brow.

"Don't surrender to self-pity. Try to master your emotions. Don't give in to anger. Say nothing to your son. Nothing conveys displeasure, sorrow more eloquently than silence. This is not a contest. It makes no sense to engage in a battle of wits with your own flesh and blood. You will only envenom the situation. Ideological quarrels do not end in victory or defeat. They persist until the rivals lay down their arms and yield to tolerance."

"But, Rabbi, my son only hears himself. He quotes from the Bible and lobs apocalyptic threats. The faith he has embraced does not tolerate dialogue, analysis, divergence. Its sole aim is to convert Jews — or consign them to Gehenna — if they resist."

"Life is a rehearsal, an improvisation," Rabbi Lazar sighed. "Your son may come to his senses one day. Or else he wandered off, never to return, in which case your wrath is wasted, and your resentment is in vain."

I can't prove it, but my son could have been the victim of a masterful psychological hijacking, not the recipient of sudden revelation. He is too intelligent to have fallen for the absurdities that he regurgitates with robot-like automatism. Nothing in his past can explain his baffling recantation. Or else, being the product of a broken home, he found no better way to get even with his ill-suited and warring parents than by disconnecting from them in a sordid annulment of his genetic, tribal, and cultural bonds, by abjuring his Jewish roots and Judaism's abstract, exquisitely vague promise of messianic deliverance, and by surrendering to a flesh-and-blood savior whose two-thousand-plus-year record of salvation has been punctuated by famine, pestilence, war, death, and damnation.

Predictably, my son created his own blend of Judeo-Christian dogmata by picking those directives and taboos that suit his self-indulgent lifestyle while snubbing those that do not. You can eat pork and still be a good Jew, he asserts in contravention of clearly stated prohibitions in Deuteronomy and Leviticus. You can ignore the Sabbath and flout Jesus' teachings on the virtues of poverty, but studying the Talmud, the primary source of Jewish religious law and theology, the centerpiece of Jewish philosophy, and the guide for the daily life of Jews — is off limits because it consists of commentaries and meditations on Jewish history, law, customs, and culture ... a sacrilege to those who consider the Bible the unredacted word of *god* and Jesus (Yeshua), who died for our sins, the redeemer of mankind who redeemed nothing. When I asked my son to itemize the things Yeshua had saved since he was martyred, and now that we live in the most ruthless, perverse, and irredeemable epoch in human history, he recited a stream of memorized — and deeply embedded — Biblical injunctions with the self-hypnotic automatism of a Bible thumper: His mouth; someone else's words.

I did briefly consider seeking help from a deprogrammer, but I decided that defection is less of a crime than self-delusion, which, in the end, exacts its own brand of retribution. I keep replaying Rabbi, Lazar's words: *"He may yet come to his senses."* Meanwhile, news from near and far remind us that religion is a divisive, partisan, exclusionary, and dangerous eccentricity; that, carried to extremes, it renders men mad and that the greatest crimes against humanity were and continue to be committed in its name.

◆◆◆

One must dare to surmise that if the Jew named Jesus had not been born, antisemitism might not have been hatched. But then someone would have had to invent the Jews, someone to blame, to hate for mankind's woes. Given a spurious pretext, often in the absence of one, anybody is liable to hate the Jews. The New Testament is filled with ludicrous Jew-hating observations and reprimands that led to sham accusations of blood libel and the wholesale massacres of Jews during nine Crusades and the *Holy* Inquisition, and which culminated in the slaughter of six million Jews, among them my paternal grandparents and two young sons.

In the Gospel of John, the foulest, most venomous antisemitic biblical tract, the word *Jews* is used sixty-three times — thirty-one times with rank hostility. No distinction is made between Jewish groups, who are all lumped together. The Sadducees, for example, prominent elsewhere, are not singularized. The enemies of Jesus are described collectively as *the Jews*, in contradistinction to the other evangelists, who do not generally blame them for the death of Jesus ... but don't express much fondness for them either. In the other three texts, the plot to put

Jesus to death is always presented as coming from a small group of priests and rulers, the Sadducees. The Gospel of John has provided antisemites with grist for their mill. It is the primary source for the image of the Jews acting collectively as the enemy of Jesus, which later became fixed in Christian minds.

Jesus' alleged words to the Jews in John (8:44), *"You are of your father the devil,"* have a sad history of horrible antisemitic re-use. They make antisemitism respectable and encourage aggression against Jews. Armed with such stimuli, pious churchgoers have considered it acceptable-- not to say their Christian duty--to join in massive attacks on Jews.

The messianic movement appeals to many types of people, but one dangerous type includes those who seek the hallowed distinction of practicing *real* Christianity. They often exhibit a mixture of self-importance and sanctimonious contempt for those pitiable *unperfected* Jews. All religions are free to present their creeds in the open market of ideas. But if they must resort to slimy tactics as the *Jews for Jesus* employ, then they obviously have nothing to offer a thinking person. This is a movement of non-Jews who pose as Jews by taking on Jewish names and faking allegiance to Judaism. They do usually have token Jewish members, who are invariably either woefully ignorant of or hostile to Judaism, or deeply delusional. They are a sham.

Much controversy abounds concerning the origins of the historical Jesus. Unfortunately, almost nothing from antiquity contains any information about his life other than the fabrications or, at best, cult-like glamorization by his biographers. No one has the slightest physical evidence to support a historical Jesus; no artifacts, lodging, works of carpentry, or self-written manuscripts. All claims about Jesus derive from texts attributed to four people, chroniclers who were not contemporaries of Jesus. There doesn't even exist a Roman record citing Pontius Pilate's involvement in the execution of a man named Jesus. The singular Jesus mentioned in Josephus' *History of Jewish Wars* seems oddly out of context and most scholars believe that early leaders of the Church, to bolster their propaganda machine and promote Jesus, inserted several improbable scenarios into their narratives. So, we are stuck with the New Testament's Four Gospels. The Books of Matthew, Luke, Mark, and John contain most of the information about the life of Jesus. These Books are not even the words of the early 1st Century Jewish-Christian sect, but rather the product of the later Greek-Christian community that authored them and lived at least two or three generations from the events they describe--way too much time for myth, legend, and shameless falsifications to intertwine with truth. More than anything, the New Testament is a polemical work with a point to prove: From the very beginning it sets out to establish, without empirical evidence, Jesus' *divinity* and messianic nature — a status he never claimed — and invent all the events in that divine mold into a religion he never intended to create. Mark, Matthew, Luke, and John were antiquity's conspiracy theorists. Messianic Judaism, Christianity's Trojan Horse, perpetuates their lies and keeps the fires of antisemitism burning.

Jewish people's subjection to Christian morality has not been universally uplifting, to say the least. What

Christians have never grasped—but Jews, even atheists like me, know intuitively—is that, longed for and eagerly awaited, the *messiah* is a sublime abstraction, an ideal, a far-flung destination reachable only at the conclusion of a righteous journey, a goal to be striven for, the romanticized but largely unachievable fusing of mankind's highest hopes and hankerings for justice and equity, an undefinable yearning that dwells in the deepest part of men's souls--not a human redeemer. Somehow, blind faith—the irrational belief in the advent of the unattainable—does not lend it legitimacy. Never did. Never will.

Pastor Mike, I am told, left his church for parts unknown. My son continues to quote John. Preaching leads naturally to inquisition, the kind so artfully honed and executed by Jesus' most loyal disciples.

THE WITCHES' HAMMER:
HERETICS, HEROES, AND SAINTS

There once was a law in Massachusetts that called for unmarried couples who lived together to be taken to the gallows, made to stand there for an hour with a rope around their necks and receive thirty-nine lashes. The 1784 decree, which prohibited couples from *"lasciviously associating and cohabitating without the benefit of marriage,"* lived in the law books until its repeal by then Governor Michael S. Dukakis in April 1987! That would not prevent the selectman of the town of Sharon, a Boston suburb, from citing the abolished blue law against Officer Linda F. Farris, 36, the first woman on the Sharon police force, and Officer Lawrence Phaneuf, 39, with whom Farris was living. In an obscene display of fake puritanism and misogyny, Farris was dismissed from the force and Phaneuf was demoted. The charges would eventually be dropped but the incident helped revive buried memories of a time when religion-mandated persecutions of suspected *sinners* reached a fever pitch in Europe and, later, in the New World.

For three centuries, the filthiest passions masqueraded under the cover of religion and man's intellect was subverted to condone bestialities that even Swift's Yahoos would blush to commit.

The record of witchcraft is horrific and vicious. Civil and church authorities swiftly and remorselessly punished *witches*, resulting in tens of thousands of innocent people being legally murdered. Judged from the ethereal heights of the preachers' pulpit, witchcraft was defined as a crime of the mind. To every theologian, judge, lawyer, Catholic or Protestant, a witch was one who, aware of god's laws, *"tries to bring about some act through an agreement with the devil."* The Jesuit demonologist, Martin Delrio (1551-1608) defined witchcraft as *"an art by which, by the power of a covenant with the devil, some wonders are wrought which defy the understanding of men."* Not to be outdone, Cotton Mather, (1663-1728), of Salem fame, the thrice-married *child prodigy* Puritan clergyman who owned at least three slaves and advocated the forced conversion of Blacks *"so that they may one day meet in heaven,"* put the American colonies on record:

> *"Witchcraft is the doing of strange and for the most part ill things by the help of evil spirits."*

It is one thing to define what the Church labeled a disease of the spirit and quite another to treat it by resorting to the unspeakable corporal therapies prescribed by the inquisitors.

♦ Repulsed by a woman to whom he made improper and unwanted advances, a German trial judge, in revenge, kidnapped her sister, accused her of witchcraft, tortured her, and burned her alive.

♦ A bishop burned more than 900 men and women, many respected and wealthy citizens as witches and confiscated their properties and estates for his own enjoyment.

♦ A French magistrate expressed remorse that instead of burning young children accused of witchcraft, he had merely sentenced them to be flogged to death while they watched their parents roast on a pyre.

♦ A Protestant minister in Scotland refused a Christian burial to a woman crushed to death by a mob because she had been accused as a witch by a sixteen-year-old lad.

♦ A woman was convicted as a witch for curing children … by washing them.

♦ Another woman was roasted as a witch for stroking a cat at an open window at the same time the householder found his brew of beer turning sour.

♦ A poor immigrant in Boston speaking only Irish and saying her prayers in Latin was branded a witch because she could not recite the Lord's prayer in English.

♦ At Salem two young men were trussed at their necks and heels until blood oozed from their noses, to force a statement used to convict suspected witches. I shall return to Salem after a brief detour in the hinterlands of religious dementia during which, every day for more than three hundred years, thousands of innocent people were humiliated, brutalized, dispossessed, and butchered.

♦♦♦

Convictions are mental prisons. They breed prejudice and encourage injustice. Institutionalized intolerance began in the 12th century and was promoted by both the Church and the state. In 1199, Pope Innocent III expanded the prohibitions against heresy and encouraged the confiscation of a heretic's possessions. The Pope's directives later became part of the Canon Law of the

Church. By a decree, *Excomunicamus,* in 1215, Innocent III forced secular authorities, on pain of heresy, *"to swear that they will strive faithfully to exterminate from their territories all heretics who have been proscribed by the Church."*

With the bull of Pope Innocent VIII in 1484, witchcraft matured. Armed with their sacred guide, the *Malleus Maleficarum* (Witches' Hammer) and with the power to torture those brought before them, inquisitors roamed Europe hunting witches. For nearly three centuries, the *Malleus* was the bible and catechism of witch hunters. Written with the encouragement of Pope Innocent VIII by Heinrich Kramer, a churchman who blamed women for his own insatiable lust (and presumed impotence), and Jacob Sprenger, a Dominican theologian and inquisitor, the *Malleus* is without question the most important and most sinister work on demonology ever written. It would help open the floodgates of inquisitorial hysteria. It sought to make effective the biblical command, *"Thou shalt not suffer a witch to live."*--Exodus (12:18).

Republished a dozen times or more, the *Malleus* became the source and inspiration for all future treatises on witchcraft. The book is divided into three parts. The first justifies the need for inquisitors to comprehend the enormity of witchcraft, which included renunciation of the Catholic faith, devotion to the devil, and carnal intercourse with incubi (male) and succubae (female) demons. Part II outlines the three types of sorcery and how they may be neutralized. Here Kramer and Sprenger describe all the doings of witches—compact with the devil, sexual relations with evil spirits, and transvection (flying on a broomstick, shovel, domestic animal, imp, or low-grade demon). That chapter also describes certain physical features characteristic of witches: Any person afflicted with a mole, cyst, scar, bunion, extra nipple of other congenital deformities was considered to have been marked by the devil and was ipso facto to be executed. An anonymous denunciation or malicious hearsay was sufficient ground to be dragged to the inquisitorial tribunal, accused of witchcraft, tortured and, after having confessed and forced to kiss the cross as an act of contrition toward god, Jesus, the Church, and all the saints in heaven, promptly consigned to the fires of hell. When they dare to confront the devil, men turn to occultism. When they fear him, they burn them. Part III of the *Malleus* lists formal rules for initiating legal action against witches, securing a conviction, and passing sentence. It concludes with the arrest, imprisonment, interrogation, and torture of witches.

The proliferation of trials for witchcraft at the end of the 16th century led to an increase in the prosecution of lycanthropy — the hallucinatory metamorphosis by which a man consumed with a sadistic craving for blood ... turns into a werewolf. The concept of metamorphosis is ancient. A Greek myth told of Lycaon, who, killed and cooked his son Nyctimus and served him to Zeus, was changed into a wolf. Plato expanded the legend: eating the flesh of a man sacrificed at that altar results in such transformation. Lycanthropy, brilliantly if bloodcurd-lingly satirized by Bram Stoker in Dracula, was not just legend or folklore. It was, just as much as witchcraft, a sin against *god*, and was even more ruthlessly punished by his earthly deputies.

◆◆◆

Were it not for the Inquisition, the demented fixations of the Catholic tribunal charged with ferreting and punishing religious heterodoxy, not a single person would have been accused of or murdered for witchcraft. Its crimes are legion. Here are, in no particular order, some of the most lurid manifestations of the *god*-inspired barbarities that fed its fires..

◆ Galileo Galilei (1564-1642) was an Italian natural philosopher, astronomer, and mathematician who made fundamental contributions to the sciences of motion, and astronomy, and to the development of the scientific method. His formulation of (circular) inertia, the law of falling bodies, and parabolic trajectories marked the beginning of a fundamental change in the study of motion. His insistence that the book of nature was written in the language of mathematics changed natural philosophy from a verbal, qualitative account to a mathematical one in which experimentation became a recognized method for discovering the facts of nature. Finally, his discoveries with the telescope revolutionized astronomy and paved the way for the acceptance of the Copernican heliocentric system—that the earth revolves around the sun, and not vice-versa. His advocacy of that system, and his rejection of Aristotelian notions about motion drew the ire of his fellow scientists and soon pissed off the princes of the Church for being in conflict with literal interpretations of scripture, and with the Ptolemaic geocentric model, which had been adopted by the Catholic Church.

On April 12, 1633, chief inquisitor Father Vincenzo

Maculano, appointed by Pope Urban VIII, launched an inquisition of Galileo and ordered the astronomer to appear in the Holy Office to begin trial. The trial of the man described by Albert Einstein as "the father of modern science," lasted three months.

Intimidated, fearing for his life, Galileo admitted that in certain parts of his book the arguments in favor of Copernicanism appeared stronger than they should have been, due to, he said, *"vain ambition, pure ignorance, and inadvertence."* On June 22, 1633, Galileo was ordered to kneel as he was found *"vehemently suspected of heresy."* He was forced to *"abandon completely the false opinion"* of Copernicanism, and to read a statement, in which he recanted much of his life's work. Aged 78, blind, and frail, he escaped the gallows and the pyre but died under house arrest.

♦ Giordano Bruno (1548-1600) was an Italian philosopher, poet, cosmological theorist and occultist. He is known for his cosmological theories, which conceptually extended to include the then novel Copernican model. He proposed that the stars were distant suns surrounded by their own planets (exoplanets), and he raised the possibility that these planets might foster life of their own, a cosmological position known as cosmic pluralism. He also insisted that the universe is infinite and could have no center. While Bruno began as a Dominican friar, he embraced Calvinism during his sojourn in Geneva. He was later tried for heresy by the Roman Inquisition on charges of denial of several core Catholic doctrines, including eternal damnation, the Trinity, the divinity of Christ, the virginity of Mary, and transubstantiation [the madcap belief that the body and blood of Christ are converted into bread and wine during Sacrament].

During the seven years of his trial in Rome, Giordano Bruno was held in confinement, lastly in the Tower of Nona. The numerous charges against him, based on some of his books as well as on witness accounts, included blasphemy, immoral conduct, and heresy in matters of dogmatic theology, and involved some of the basic doctrines of his philosophy and cosmology.

Bruno defended himself, insisting that he accepted the Church's dogmatic teachings, but trying to preserve the basis of his cosmological views. His trial was overseen by the Inquisitor Cardinal Bellarmine, who demanded a full recantation, which Bruno eventually refused. On 20 January 1600, Pope Clement VIII declared Bruno a heretic, and the Inquisition issued a sentence of death. According to the correspondence of Gaspar Schopp, a German Catholic polemicist, Bruno is said to have made a threatening gesture towards his judges and to have replied: *Maiori forsan cum timore sententiam in me fertis quam ego accipiam* [*"Perhaps you pronounce this sentence against* me *with greater fear than I receive it."*] He was turned over to the secular authorities. On 17 February 1600, in the Campo de' Fiori (a central Roman market square), with his *"tongue imprisoned because of his wicked words,"* Bruno was stripped naked and hung upside down before being burned alive at the stake. His ashes were thrown into the Tiber River. All of Bruno's works were placed on the Vatican's Index of prohibited books in 1603. Bruno is a symbol for free thought and speech in present-day Rome, where an annual memorial service takes place close to the spot where he was executed.

◆   Girolamo Savonarola (1452-1498) was an ascetic Italian Dominican and proto-Protestant friar and a preacher active in Renaissance Florence. He became known for his prophecies of civic glory, and his calls for Christian renewal. He denounced clerical corruption, despotic rule, and the exploitation of the poor. Without mentioning names, he made pointed allusions to tyrants who usurped the freedom of the people, and he excoriated their allies, the rich and powerful who neglected and exploited the poor. Complaining of the evil lives of a corrupt clergy, he now called for repentance and renewal before the imminent arrival of a divine scourge. Savonarola never abandoned the dogmas of the Roman Catholic Church; for example, he held to a belief in seven sacraments and that the Church of Rome is *"the mother of all other churches and the pope its head."* However his relentless protests against papal corruption, reliance on the Bible as the main guide have linked Savonarola with the later reformation. He held scripture as a very high authority, stating: *"I preach the regeneration of the Church, taking the Scriptures as my sole guide."*

On 12 May 1497, Pope Alexander VI charged Savonarola with heresy and sedition. He excommunicated him for describing the Church as a whore and threatened his followers with an interdict if they persisted in harboring him. On 18 March 1498, after much debate and steady pressure from a worried government, Savonarola withdrew from public preaching. Under the stress of excommunication, he composed his spiritual masterpiece, the *Triumph of the Cross*, a celebration of the victory of the Cross over sin and death and an exploration of what it means to be a Christian. Under torture Savonarola confessed to having invented his prophecies and visions, then recanted, then confessed again. In his prison cell he composed meditations on Psalms 51 and 31. On the morning of 23 May 1498, he was led out into the main square where, before a tribunal of high clerics and government officials, he was condemned as a heretic and schismatic, and sentenced to die forthwith. Stripped of his Dominican garments in ritual degradation, he mounted the scaffold in his thin white shirt. He was hanged, while a fire was lit under him. To prevent devotees from sifting for relics, his ashes were carted away and scattered in the Arno River.

How ironic—and characteristic of the savage and vindictive nature of religion—that Savonarola was martyred for revering and upholding Christianity's most sacred doctrines.

• Joan of Arc (1412-1431). Claiming to be acting under divine guidance, La Pucelle d'Orléans [the virgin of Orléans] became a military leader who transcended gender roles and gained recognition as a savior of France. The literature of Joan of Arc exceeds 5,000 items. The New York Public Library catalogues some 700 entries but only one (a magazine) mentions witchcraft. It is often assumed that she was tried as a witch. This is inaccurate. This young girl of peasant origins was popularly rumored to be a sorceress but officially accused by the Church of apostasy for insisting that she had received from saints Michael, Margaret of Antioch, and Catherine of

Alexandria the mission to deliver France from the occupying English. She would be burned at the stake as a relapsed heretic.

She joined the future King Charles VII, led his troops victoriously against the English armies, lifting the siege of Orleans, securing Charles' coronation, in Reims, and helping to reverse the course of the Hundred Years War. Captured in 1430 by the Burgundians as she tried to lift the siege of Compiegne, she was sold to the English for the sum of ten thousand pounds. Three days later, Bishop Pierre Cauchon, a renegade cleric acting on behalf of the English, claimed episcopal jurisdiction over Joan *"as one violently suspect of several errors savoring heresy,"* and accusing her of sorcery and invocation of demons. She was imprisoned in a castle in Rouen. En route, she was exhibited in a specially constructed iron cage, barely large enough for her to stand upright, chained by the neck, hands, and feet. Interrogated by forty-two priests, Joan insisted that the voices from saints Michael, Catherine, and Margaret were divine ... which the Church chose to attribute ... to the devil.

Excommunicated, the 20-year-old girl, her head crowned with a miter reading *"Relapsed heretic, apostate, idolater,"* was placed high on the pyre so the flames would reach her slowly. She was burned alive in 1431 after a heresy trial led by Bishop Cauchon, the former rector of the University of Paris. Tainted by numerous irregularities, this trial saw its revision ordered by Pope Callistus III in 1455. A second trial was conducted which concluded, in 1456, that Joan was innocent. In 1904 Joan was deemed *"venerable"* by Pope Pius X and beatified in

1908. Canonized in 1920, Joan of Arc became one of France's patron saints nearly five centuries after her horrific ordeal. She has since come to symbolize, as many of the Inquisition's crimes attest, a victim of religion muscling in on the body politic—later justified as the *"intimate union between patriotism and the Catholic faith."*

It is interesting to note that hegemonic and dynastic interests—as was the case when Catholic Mary Queen of Scots was executed in 1587 on orders of her cousin, the Protestant Queen Elizabeth I—are justifiably seen as a clash between religions rather than politics.

◆ The Salem Witch Trials (1692-1693). *"So horrid and hellish is the crime of witchcraft, that were god's thoughts our thoughts. or god's way our ways, it could be no other but unpardonable."* So wrote Cotton Mather (1662-1728), a lasting example of the wickedness and harm that sincere, if misguided, god-fearing people can cause when religious fanaticism subverts reason. The year 1692 seems to have been a particularly troubled one in New England, It was a time of political turmoil, with Increase Mather, Cotton's father, at the English court seeking clarification of the colony's status. The French were waging war and the native tribes were on the warpath. Taxes were intolerable, winters were long and cruel, pirates were masters of the sea, and smallpox was raging. To folks brought up in a restricting evangelical world, all their woes were caused by the devil and his agents on earth: witches. Belief in the supernatural was widespread and unquestioned. The Bible was the word of god and the word of god turned legend into the theocratic law of the land. Any traffic with Satan was treason toward god—

and the colony. This religious control of the state accounts for the panic in Massachusetts at a time when the witchcraft delusion was waning. When on January 13, 1693, a certain William Barker confessed to being a witch, formal charges against him read that he:

> *"mallitiously and felloniously A Covenant with the Devill did make, And did Signe the Devills Booke with Blood, and gave himselfe Soule & body to the Devil…"*

…for the purpose of destroying Salem Village, abolishing the Church of *god* and setting up Satan's kingdom. It is widely suspected that Barker had been falsely accused by unnamed persons and that, as was widely the case during the Inquisition, he had in turn been forced to name others. English writer, John Evelyn (1620-1706), recorded in his diary:

> *"Unheard stories of the universal increase of witches in New England; men, women, and children devoting themselves to the Devil, so as to threaten the subversion of the government."*

The instigators of this subversion turned out to have been a group of unmarried young women who visited Rev. Samuel Parris to listen to his West Indian slave Tituba's tales of voodoo, evil spirits, and lycanthropes [werewolves]. Parris' daughter, Elizabeth, age 9 and her cousin, Abigail Williams, 11, were so emotionally excited, coming at the onset of puberty, that they went into fits of uncontrollable sobbing, and convulsions.

Make a very long and ugly story short, the hysteria spread through genteel Salem like the clap at a bacchanale. About 140 individuals, men and women, were brought to trial and formally charged with witchcraft. Among them, 31 were condemned to death, of whom 19 were hanged, one was *"pressed"* to death, and two died in prison. As Charles W. Upham (1802-1875) U.S. Representative from Massachusetts and the seventh mayor of Salem, wrote in his two-volume *Salem Witchcraft*:

> *"Error is seldom overthrown by mere reasoning. It yields only to the logic of events. No power of learning or wit could have rooted the witchcraft superstition out of the minds of men. Nothing short of a demonstration of their deformities, follies and horrors, such as here was held up to the view of the world, could have given their death blow. This was the final cause of Salem witchcraft and makes it one of the great landmarks in the world's history."*

After the mid-1800s, there were no more reports of witches being sacrificed but attempts to hassle people accused of *blighting* cattle and crops with the *evil eye* lingered for another decade or so.

◆◆◆

Belief in witchcraft, while less widespread than four centuries ago, is still alive today. The witches themselves are the shadowy figures the Church and fascist states surveil, harass, intimidate and attempt to silence-- incorruptible and outspoken members of the press, gadflies, mudslingers, busybodies, purveyors of fake news, agents of social discontent, blabbermouths who threaten the established order, the so-called enemies of the people. Who can forget the wave of hysteria that led to the unlawful internment of German- and Japanese- Americans? Or the panic that swept over the rapidly industrializing U.S. in the aftermath of the First World War, when leftist thinking radicals, called anarchists, were demanding fair wages, shorter workdays, and a 40-hour work week? Any anti-capitalism talk automatically meant support for a *communist* state.

And who among those of us old enough to remember, doesn't shudder at the inquisitorial McCarthy-era House Committee on Un-American Activities created in 1938 to investigate alleged disloyalty and subversive activities on the part of private citizens, public employees, and organizations suspected of having subversive ties. In 1947, the committee held nine days of hearings into alleged *communist* propaganda and influence in the Hollywood motion picture industry. After conviction on contempt of Congress charges for refusal to answer some questions posed by committee members, the Hollywood Ten were blacklisted by the industry. Eventually, more than 300 artists — including directors, radio commentators, actors, and particularly screenwriters — were boycotted by the studios. Some, like Charlie Chaplin, Orson Welles, Alan Lomax, Paul Robeson, and Yip Harburg, left the U.S. or went underground to find work. Others like Dalton Trumbo wrote under pseudonyms or the names of colleagues. Only about ten percent succeeded in rebuilding careers within the entertainment industry. Although he was never called before McCarthy's demented tribunal, Frank Capra was suspected of harboring leftists views. Speaking against capitalism and advocating for workers' rights is still seen as anti-American.

Last, *The Lavender Scare* of the 1950s was a hysterical

witch hunt targeting homosexual U.S. government employees and warning of the security risks they might present. All were fired. This *moral panic* contributed to and paralleled the anti-*communist* campaign known as McCarthyism and the Second Red Scare. Gay men and lesbians were said to be *communist* sympathizers. It was thought that gay people were more susceptible to being manipulated, which could pose a threat to the country. Lesbians were at less risk of persecution than gay men, but some lesbians were interrogated and lost their jobs. *The Lavender Scare* normalized persecution of homosexuals through the bureaucratic institutionalization of homophobia.

All witch hunts are inquisitorial in character and can be said to be religious in origin, flavor, and intent as they profess to be inspired by morality and intended to cleanse society from sin. As such, and as are all faith-based precepts, they are the essence of evil. It's bad enough to be lied to. It's humiliating when liars make no effort to render their lies believable. To explain evil is to trivialize it. I shall not try.

LET US PREY

In the age of extinction, we are told, only love remains. Are we capable of loving indiscriminately? Or do we reserve our affection and loyalty for those closest to us? We hear love being preached in houses of worship, these temples of mendacity where the fears and obsessions and hopes and chimeras that haunt us are staged to induce jubilant hysteria or mournful self-contemplation. And we know that when the waving, trembling outstretched arms that reach skyward come down, when the last amen and the final breathless hallelujahs have been uttered, when feverish eyes that glimpsed the face of *god* and sought salvation in a trance-like moment of ecstasy have reopened, the faithful, these pious souls, these model citizens, their ears still ringing from some exalted homily or sacred hymn, will reconnect with the profane world from which they come and the guzzling, the fornicating, the indiscriminate breeding, the gossiping, the hatred, the lying, the killing will resume.

I am not without empathy, but the feeling is abstract, not visceral. I'd be a liar if I claimed that I can love anyone beyond the people in my life. And I'm not even sure it's love. Age, I discover, has spawned a persistent but guiltless repugnance toward all manners of distractions and irritants that have earned me, in turn, the resentment, if not the hostility of those not bothered by what I abohr: noise; traffic; slow drivers; homicidal/suicidal drivers; people who talk too much; people who talk with their hands; busybodies and know-it-alls; chauvinists and flag-waivers; selfie-takers; soccer moms; mystics and religious zealots; cheerleaders and motivational speakers; military parades; the Second Amendment; the Electoral College; spelling bees; televangelists; hog-calling contests; Tupperware parties; rodeos; football and rugby (violence and mayhem for the sake of violence and mayhem); wrestling (the vulgar, violent simulation of violence); NASCAR (noise and violence on wheels); hunting and bullfighting; people who start a sentence with *So* when nothing preceding it suggests consequence or disclosure; teens who insert *like* six times in a seven-word sentence; old women who dress like Shirley Temple and paint their upper lip crimson red; golf, one of the most inane pastimes ever conceived; smart phones and the boors who use them in public; the hoity-toity pedants who like to say, *at the end of the day*, when what they mean is *ultimately*, not late afternoon, evening, dusk, twilight, sunset or the dead of night; and the morons who insist, *"I'm entitled to my opinions"* — an incongruity with which any opposition to an absurd idea is put down by pretending that one has the right to disfigure the truth. It is uttered out of ignorance or stupidity or, more wickedly, to defend factually indefensible positions. However irrational or insensitive these aversions might be, I shall not part with them. They enliven my existence.

Love? My friend Kulbir, a devout Sikh, says that the Gurus' wisdom can help turn ordinary humans into kind and virtuous beings. I know him to be a righteous man. Having perused the Guru Granth Sahib, Sikhism's sacred scriptures, I recognize in Kulbir the incarnated emissary of teachings that promote equality among all races irrespective of caste, religion, color, status, age, or gender, that value positive ideals like truth, empathy, contentment, humility, and love, and that decry the inner evils of lust, anger, greed, material attachment, and ego. I asked Kulbir: Do humans have value? He found the question both absurd and odious. Kulbir put his faith in the ferryman and crossed the river unscathed. He found his place. I'm still struggling to keep afloat in its raging current.

◆◆◆

Religious faith is taught, imprinted, sometimes even beaten into children born with a clean slate and lacking fear or preconceptions. I don't believe in a *god* gene (the reductionist theory that human spirituality is influenced by heredity and that a specific gene predisposes humans towards spiritual or mystic experiences). Taken to extremes, religion acquires all the characteristics of full-blown psychosis. Even Kulbir grudgingly concedes that religious fanaticism is what led to the assassination of India's Prime Minister, Indira Gandhi by her two Sikh bodyguards in 1984 and that separatist fervor continues to feed the centuries-old sectarian hatreds that prevent Sikhs, Hindus, ad Muslims from ever seeing eye to eye.

About 85 percent of humans believe in a pantheon of gods. The most popular is an invisible, deaf, mute (but omnipotent) spirit inhabiting the nether regions of the cosmos and ready to consign the faithful for the slightest peccadillo to the infernal depths of perdition. Others, transmuted into *saints*, are carved out of wood, sculpted in granite, or marble, molded from clay, fashioned from papier mâché and garishly painted. In his masterful *The Discovery of France*, British author and literary critic, Graham Robb (1958-) recounts an incident during which

French villagers were upset when the curé [priest] *"tried to replace a filthy, shapeless, and partially incinerated lump of wood with a shiny new saint fresh from the factory."*

Other *gods* are yet unseen but said to be perched on the highest mountains, inhabiting the deepest lakes and haunting the most impenetrable forests. Many people also believe that once they trash this planet and die, they will be transported to a better place that they will likely proceed to vandalize. Religion has been fostering apocalypse as a logical end of its world model and earthly existence, and generations have been raised to invoke it, not to prevent it. Would *god* be willing to create another world for us if we fail to save this one? He'd be a fool if he did.

If we can blame one institution for our mental decrepitude and looming demise it's not (only) the banks, corporations, gun merchants, and crooked politicians. It's religion, the exploitation and emotional enslavement of men by instilling the concept of guilt, retribution, and immortality. Said Robert Ingersoll (1833-1899):

"Religion supports nobody. It has to be supported, it is a perpetual mendicant. It lives on the labors of others, and then has the arrogance to pretend that it supports the giver."

Whereas enlightenment is a state of mental illumination that transcends dogma and rigid ideas, religions, all concocted in the same fiction-producing crucible, are the single greatest obstacles to the kind of tolerance and open-mindedness that the enlightened among us radiate. Religion is divisive and exclusionary, and a major source of conflict. More blood has been shed in its name than any other cause.

There are about 150 established religions, each insisting it has a direct Hypertext Transfer Protocol link to *god*. If that's not against the laws of physics, I don't know what is. But then again, there is nothing logical about religion ... which is why illogical humans still believe in fairytales — the literary kind and their politicized variants. Everywhere, all I see is greed, selfishness, concupiscence, indifference, hypocrisy, corruption, and folly.

I've known pious people of every faith. Underneath the ecstasy, the jubilation, and the hallelujahs lurk dark fears and self-doubts and unanswered prayers that the faithful awkwardly attribute to *god's strange and mysterious ways*. Most corrosive is the subconscious fear of lapsing convictions, an-ever present state of mind that sends the faithful to extremes of religiosity — ritualistic, robotic, frenzied. Such people are to be pitied because that's all they have. What appears to be euphoria is in fact externalized anxiety.

I have also known people who never go to synagogue, church, mosque or gurudwara but who quietly, anonymously, invoke some undefinable energy source in the temple of their own mind. For others, religion without histrionics is meaningless. The Mass and frenzied revivalist rituals are stirring reminders of the grandiose power of staged mysticism. It's free entertainment.

For two thousand years earthlings have been waiting for the end of the world and the Second Landing. It did not happen. The navigator plotted the wrong course, got lost, and slammed the vessel into a razor-sharp shallow reef. Religion asserts that a talking monkey has transcendental worth in the Universe. While a talking monkey is an interesting phenomenon—though not as innocent or deserving of mercy as the great apes that preceded him—his worth has been seriously overestimated. He is dangerous enough in the buff. Armed with *god* (and his indispensable firearms) he becomes criminally insane. Love thy neighbor? Very noble advice when the neighbor is one of us. Otherwise, it's rubbish. It is much easier to hate than to love. Just look around.

◆◆◆

America has a long tradition of religious fundamentalism and fanaticism. The first settlers believed in witches and brought them to trial. To force a confession of heresy and witchcraft, they tormented them. We now know how the Holy Inquisition, which endured well into the mid-19th century, was involved in the institutionalization of witchcraft and how it was able to create witchcraft where it did not exist by means of torture, shrewd interrogation techniques, and mental cruelty. The last person to be executed by the Inquisition was Cayetano Ripoll, a Spanish schoolmaster hanged for heresy in 1826. The fears such methods inspired were reinforced by fiery Sunday and feast-day sermons. Didn't the book of Apocalypse predict that the coming of the Antichrist would be heralded by great swarms of heretics and witches?

When the Puritans, all good Christians, were not hunting witches, they were also busy massacring *Injuns* in *god*'s name. Small towns and rural areas remain to this day bastions of fanatical religiosity. I once attended (as an uninvolved spectator…) a charismatic Christian revivalist service, a free-for-all affair during which people faint, jump up and down like demented macaques, babble incoherently, weep uncontrollably, handle deadly snakes, and throw themselves into the arms of the pastor — generally a vile con man who drives home to his multi-million-dollar mansion in his Rolls Royce, both the earthly rewards his flock's blessed largesse enables him to acquire and enjoy. After all, money is good, he tells his flock:

"Regardless of what you may have been taught, god wants you to be rich so that you may enjoy the good things money can buy, and because it is divinely right for you to be rich."

Belief in witchcraft, while less widespread than five centuries ago, is still alive today. Witch hunts, as did those set off by Senator Joe McCarthy's hysterical rants, continue to target *communists,* atheists, purveyors of fake news, and enemies of the people, a coterie of exasperated, truth-telling rebels who keep warning that, if we let them, book-burning inquisitors, mind-manipulating mega-lomaniacs, and body snatchers now incubating in their pods — in Congress, churches, schools, all copiously irrigated by social media — will bury us all in the catacombs of truth, justice, and reason.

ENDGAME

In the beginning was the Age of Innocence. The world was neither formless nor empty. It's just that man, the last in a series of random transmutations from great ape to anthropoid had not yet risen from four- to two-legged locomotion and begun to reign over the fish in the sea, the birds in the sky, the livestock, all the wild animals on the earth, and the small animals that scurry along the ground, nor to wreak havoc upon the realm. Then, one day, as dawn ascended, the bipedal creatures picked up a rock, a bough, a bone. They felt a strange power surging through their fists and the carnage began. At high noon they began lobbing bombs. Fragmentation bombs rip, slash, shred. Incendiary bombs scorch. Concussion bombs produce shock waves that shatter granite. Napalm, like molten lead, sticks to flesh and devours it. Some bombs spread the plague. Others paralyze, suffocate, blind. Neutron bombs snuff out lives but spare monuments and shrines. Future munitions will target the poor, the sick, the mad. Some will be programmed to obliterate certain races. Skunk works might even be developing death-dealing ordnance that wipes out all graying men who engage in belligerent banter and who can't help but feel that more bombs are on the way, who say so out loud and who warn that there will soon be no good place on earth to hide, not in a synagogue, church or mosque, because being poltroons, Yahweh, Theos, and Allah have long since absconded from these sacred sanctuaries for fear that they might be asked to perform miracles..

As I surveyed the world from the unobstructed

heights of lived experience, I was also reminded that planet Earth is a place where some have more than anyone could ever need to live with dignity, while others have nothing. It's a realm in which good and evil are hotly contested and narrowly interwoven, where right and wrong feed upon each other with such voracity that neither wins nor loses so that both may emerge unscathed from their unholy symbiosis. It's a locale where a corrupt, craven, avaricious gerontocracy calls upon the very young to risk mutilation and insanity and to die in their stead. It's a place where wars are waged to break the monotony of peace, where combatants are feted for their battlefield homicidal deeds with medals and ribbons and boisterous pageants, whereas common felons rot in stinking jails or swing from the gallows or fry on the electric chair. It's the halfway house where, left to their own devices, flawed but redeemable beings mutate into a race of cutthroats. It's the purgatory where a species of erect bipedal primates was exiled a quarter of a million years ago so that they might expiate their brutish ways. Instead, they went to war to wrest the *Holy Land* from the apostate Jews and Muslims. They burned Giordano Bruno, Girolamo Savonarola, and Jacques de Molay alive for contradicting the Church's grotesque beliefs and ruthless mandates. Convicted as a *heretic,* a label still used today to brand skeptics and truth-tellers, Joan of Arc suffered the same fate, only to be later beatified and canonized a *saint* by the same thugs who ordered her execution. Galileo Galilei, who championed Copernican heliocentrism (the Earth revolves round the Sun, not the other way around) was forced by the Inquisition to recant and died under house arrest a broken man. In an important sense, which can never impugn his genius or diminish his scientific achievements, the trial of Galileo is fascinating for the insights it provides into the inner workings of intolerance—be it the Inquisition, the efficient, ruthless tribunal from whose diabolical secret procedures no one escaped unscathed once its wrath was aroused—or today's political fanaticism, bigotry, and religious extremism.

Inquisitors also burned books. Works by Europe's intellectual elites, among them Erasmus, Machiavelli, Dante, Voltaire, Rousseau, Descartes, Leibnitz, Spinoza, and Bocaccio—later Balzac, Dumas, Flaubert, Hugo, Sartre, and Zola—were repugnant to the Church and banned. Censorship, redaction, and expurgation had a disastrous effect on the development of scientific thought, philosophy, and art, as it does now in parts of the world where freethinking, erudition, and tolerance, the cardinal virtue of righteous men, are considered unpatriotic or treasonous. It wasn't until 1966 that the Congregation for the Doctrine of the Faith abolished the Index, a list of publications deemed heretical, satanic, or contrary to morality, conceding that while the list maintained its moral force by teaching Christians to beware of writings that could dilute or extinguish their faith, it was no longer able to enforce it. Remarking on the fragility of religious faith and the lengths to which the Church would go to enforce it, Aldous Huxley warned:

> *"The Inquisition burns and tortures in order to perpetuate a creed, a ritual, and an ecclesiastico-politico-financial organization regarded as necessary to man's salvation."*

Huxley's words were prophetic in the omens they

contained: the rise of radicalism and prejudice, and the methods intolerant people devise to maintain their supremacy and protect the bounties their extremism bestows in a society seduced to believe that deity, private enterprise, and *personal initiative* without limits or controls provide the greatest opportunity for happiness ... as they cling to the belief that since nothing can prevent the existence of an all-seeing, all-knowing *supreme being* endowed with infinite attributes, it follows that, out of necessity, such a being must exist. That's one way of elevating absurdity to an elysian finale.

◆◆◆

Everybody has opinions. Naïve or wacky, they are easily deconstructed and dismissed. Inflexible or toxic, they blind us, inflate us with arrogance. Taken to the extreme, they can drive us mad. Opining from emotion does the truth a disservice. It just makes us feel better about ourselves because, heavens forbid, we should be wrong about anything that comes out unreflexively out of our mouths. And yet, opinions are the wooden stakes with which monstrous truths are often sacrificed. Without them there would be nothing to talk about. It's not a question of semantics or the ambiguities of personal perception. Clearly, an opinion is universally understood as a view or judgment formed about something, but it is not necessarily based on fact or empirical knowledge. When we opine, we express a feeling, an attitude, a sentiment, not a fact. Whether a statement is a fact or an opinion depends on the validity of the statement. Fact refers to something true or real, which is backed by evidence, observation, documentation. Newton's law of

149

gravity wasn't based on an opinion or hearsay. It was a deduction grounded on study and repeatable experiments. When Einstein formulated his relativity theories, he wasn't hypothesizing; his was a conclusion based on the totality of certain scientific facts that have since been vindicated. $E=mc^2$ is not an opinion; it's an empirical reality.

Opinions are rarely original. We adopt them, we cling to them because independent and critical reasoning require an enormous capital of intellectual latitude, courage, and moral honesty, not to mention a bundle of gray matter uncontaminated by immovable beliefs. Instead, we shamelessly peddle them while being convinced of our own infallible deductive faculties. The great tragedy is that few among us care about the lies that opinions conceal. They are the dungeons in which we lock ourselves by feigning a clear conscience — more often than not the result of a faulty memory. Most of our beliefs are built on a vast scaffolding of dogmas, doctrines, acquired prejudices, and chimeras that are always advanced by someone else. And yet we believe that they are the fruit of our own ruminations because they protect us from what we fear most: reality. No, *god* did not create the heavens and the earth in six days and rested on the seventh. Let's be serious: Moses did not part the Red Sea. Jesus was not born by parthenogenesis. Elvis is not alive. The Holocaust is not a myth. The Moon landing was not faked. The CIA did not have a hand in JFK's assassination. The 9/11 attack was not an inside job perpetrated by Jews. Top Democrats are not behind a child sex ring (though many priests have been…) The Earth is not flat. and my all-time favorite, COVID-19 is not an attempt at population control. (During the Holy Inquisition, Jews were accused of poisoning wells and causing the Black Death). Today we are accused of starting wildfires with "space lasers," a fantasy concocted by an ignorant, wicked idiot — Congresswoman Marjorie Taylor Greene ... and regurgitated by other imbeciles.

At best, opinions impart second-hand views endlessly retold, recast, and misread: the idiosyncratic, hand-me-down, robotic indoctrinations to which we are subject from the youngest age; the lies our parents feed us; the expedient reinterpretations of history; the often-slanted pedagogy of our teachers; the absurd credos of religion; the partisan reflections of party politics. At worst, cleverly packaged, cunningly marketed, opinions masquerading as fact (or Gospel truth ...) have the power to anesthetize or agitate men, lead them to the kind of mass frenzy and violence to which History has been witness.

We all need to hear stories. But, somehow, we're fond only of those that don't dispute our own accounts of reality, that don't threaten our ideological or emotional comfort zones. We don't bother to read between the lines. We refuse to extricate fact from cautionary tale. We allow hints of veracity — or out-and-out lies to color our fantasies, to stimulate our adrenal glands — we're thrilled by the oblique suggestion of danger, horror, or salaciousness so long as these enticements remain abstract, so long as we're surrogates, vicarious onlookers, not partakers. Other people's stories help legitimize our voyeurism. The tales we spin betray our narcissism.

◆ ◆ ◆

Two years ago I was invited to address a group of high school seniors who'd expressed an interest in pursuing a career in journalism. I had planned to preface my presentation, which included what I'd been taught at the Paris University School of Journalism and what I'd learned along the way, by asking two questions, the first speculative, the second practical: What is the truth; and how does one conclude that something is true.

Then came the Covid pandemic and the invitation was wisely withdrawn. I called the teacher and suggested that her students submit their answers by e-mail. They did. Three of the four similarly — and unimaginatively — characterized the truth as "the lessons my parents impart;" "what the Holy Bible teaches;" "what our pastor preaches; and "the word of *god.*" The same three were unable to lucidly answer the second question. Given their age and allegedly excellent academic record, I was disappointed but hardly shocked.

The lone exception, a young woman of 18, acknowledged that the truth *"is too broad, too personal, too elusive, too shifting a concept to be accurately or fairly defined, but that it can easily be recognized when empirically demonstrated."*

I recommended that she be encouraged to apply to journalism school. I told the teacher that I did not expect the others to embrace a craft premised on the ceaseless pursuit and cold-blooded exhumation of glaring facts from a mass grave of lies. I was not surprised to learn that the three had since opted to pursue other careers and that the lone exception had been enrolled at the S. I.

Newhouse Communications complex now part of the Syracuse University School of Journalism whose inauguration I attended and reported on in 1964.

IN HIS OWN IMAGE

It had never been done. It would never be tried again. Not even in a dream. Here was an unrepeatable chance event that upended the laws of potentiality and defied the very core of reason. Bear with me. Imagine absurdity challenging the sublime. Picture the unthinkable. And yet, against all odds, preposterous as it sounds, it happened. A driving force heretofore unimagined, the offspring of a staggering abstraction that can't be annulled once spawned — nor left untested — burst out of a single, indissoluble vanishing point. So they said.

Reaching into nonexistence (or emerging from it?), now ponderable if not fully manifest, suspended somewhere between immanence and inscrutability (as are all things when first caused) *he* endowed *himself* with being. In a single surge of cognition, exceeding *his* creative potential, *he* was now *his* own fait accompli, his own irreversible magnum opus. *He* had just invented *himself.* Are still with me?

Free from *his* cerebral cocoon, fully transfigured from genderless ambiguity to virile causality, *he* surveyed *his* completeness. Heeding a time of *his* own calibration, anxious to add purpose to will, meaning to intent, momentum to stimulus, *he* separated cause from effect, quintessence from nonconformity, provenance from possibility, state from circumstance, identity from distinction, metaphor from divergence. In short, *he* elaborated all manner of paradox and contrariety which would forever set *him* apart from those who are not and can never be *him*.

To avert any confusion between *him* and the teeming realm *his* incarnation might evoke, *he* relinquished form for unquantifiable symmetry; *he* traded transparency for impenetrability. *His* whole would be indivisible yet limitless, here brimming with presence, there immersed in a desolation so vast that even time would stand still at points unmarked and of *his* own geometry. *He* then granted *himself* the capacity to remain unmoved by sorrow and calamity. To justify such dispassion, *he* endowed himself with ostensible kindness and discernible cruelty, allowing *himself* to be perceived as possessing equal doses of benevolence and evil, munificence and malice, genius and imbecility, as circumstances dictated, and depending upon the prevailing mood and attitudes *he* instilled.

Now armed with an ego, *he* gave *himself* an indecipherable forename by which others would know *him*. Some followed *him* in silent awe. Others, whose cries were never heard, wept and suffered and died forgotten because pain, by some outlandish precept, is the path out of bondage. *His* ear inattentive and his breast unfaithful to the throngs who called on *him* and sought *his* succor, *he* was forgotten, in time, like a distant tragedy, like a bad dream.

Cynics suggest that *he*'d been the figment of *his* own imagination. Others, with greater forbearance, speculated that, in a supreme act of mercy, having lost faith in *his* own inflated image, using *his* extraordinary powers, *he* nullified himself for the good of all.

A great, raging, thunderous roar shook *his* domain, And the legend, so carefully crafted, preserved, and perpetuated, was soon forgotten. No one knows for sure whether *he* was insane or whether those *he* entrapped had lost all reason. And peace eternal reigned at last upon the gullible remnant few left to ponder the incongruity of being *god*.

RECTAL VENTRILOQUISM

Since time immemorial, idealists raised their voices against greed, corruptibility, absurd beliefs, decadence, and inhumanity. History 101. Nothing changed. The Jew named Jesus was crucified, not for denying Judaism's ethics but for wanting to enforce them. Carthusian monks have been praying for peace since a disgruntled priest named Bruno and twelve followers fed up with the venal ways of the Church retreated to a monastery in the French Alps in 1084. Their prayers remain unheard and unheeded to this day, evidence that prayer has no effect on the physical world. Galileo was tried by the Inquisition and died under house arrest for insisting that the Earth is round and that it revolves around the Sun, not the other way around. Countless dreamers have been martyred for preaching love, equality, and justice, or for telling inconvenient truths. Wasn't I targeted for assassination some thirty years ago and didn't I have to abscond in the middle of the night when I identified the killers of a young Mayan tribal chieftain (he was shot, stabbed, *and* scalped) who called for the return of ancestral lands stolen by white settlers? Weren't millions of Native Americans massacred so that intruders could spread out over their domains and enjoy "life, liberty, and the pursuit of happiness"? Weren't Gandhi and Martin Luther King slain for preaching non-violence? What about 250 years of slavery and another few decades of Jim Crow in an America that, to this day, has the audacity to proclaim itself righteous and a model for the world? Weren't Lincoln, John F. Kennedy, and his brother Robert killed for their *progressive* views? Wasn't Nelson Mandela imprisoned for 27 years for defying South Africa's brutal apartheid regime? Aren't Russian dissidents targeted for death (and dying) as we speak? Isn't Ukraine being reduced to rubble as civilian casualties continue to rise?

The dawn of Homo sapiens as an *improved* offshoot of the great apes suggests a gradual makeover from one species to another, both sharing huge amounts of DNA and strikingly similar anatomical features. One must be blind or stubborn to deny that we look alike. But that's where the similarities end. Somewhere along the way, defying conventional physics, evolution made a sudden and radical turn. Homo sapiens spawned Socrates and Attila, Shakespeare and Hitler, Galileo and Torquemada, Einstein and Trump, whereas unpretentious and guileless, fated for extinction, the gentle gorillas and self-effacing orangutans are at peace with nature and enjoying their now foreshortened solitary existence.

The insurrection I have been advocating all these years calls for a moral and intellectual transformation of man, not a blood-soaked upheaval. But that too is a quixotic, unachievable goal. Man does not and will not change. And the little planet that we continue to plunder and deface will do just fine after the last Cain slays the last Abel. We are not *god's* most perfect creation. We are a freak of evolution and nature will sooner or later exact its rightful revenge upon the flawed creatures that spurn it. The sooner the better because what we face ahead will be

W. E. Gutman

unendurable. *Homo hominis lupus* [Man is a wolf to man].*

With sincere apologies to wolves.

◆◆◆

So, in parting, for the last time, I ask: Where is *god* when men betray each other, when they are lied to by their leaders, when they are crucified, burned at the stake, hanged from the tallest trees, enslaved, humiliated, starved, maimed and killed on distant battlefields, wiped out by ghastly plagues and pulverized by unforgiving natural cataclysms,? Where was this all-merciful *god* when his *Chosen People*, now living in the very domain *he* granted them, were overwhelmed, tortured, raped, decapitated, and executed last October as they slept, by bloodthirsty thugs obeying their own *god*'s demented commands? What does *he* have to say to those who weep at the carnage (more than 1,200 dead at this writing) while they silently and justifiably curse *his* obscene indifference?

But alright. I get it. It has been postulated, without a shred of empirical evidence but with colossal effrontery that *god*, the so-called *supreme reality*, is that *thing* (?) which can only be apprehended by thought, not objective experience, that, stupefyingly, although *he* was invented by man, *he* exists independently of human perception, that self-imposed neutrality prevents *him* from taking part or interfering in human affairs, that, being an abstraction incapable of being known, only inferred, *he* must remain

---

* *Democracy* is an imperfect and ultimately self-destructive system of governance. So long as it tolerates the existence and proliferation of undemocratic ideas, people, and institutions, it is powerless against those who would threaten to dismantle it.

159

unknowable and therefore needs no explanation because doing so trivializes *him*.

ARE YOU KIDDING ME? Such rectal ventriloquism leaves me speechless. Hard as I try, I cannot conceive of an intuitive process which would lead me to conclude—should I be allowed to lean on logic alone—and by such process, to believe in the existence of an all-seeing but inscrutable, invisible, indecipherable, incomprehensible being spawned by fear, molded by superstition, and sustained by man's primeval compulsion to be surveilled, humbled, and chastised for being imperfect. What I will concede is that nature created man in an infinite variety of specimens whereas man, lacking nature's boundless imagination—and for the sake of parsimony—created *god*, the unseen, inaccessible, absentee landlord, the unresponsive, petulant ghost that rules heaven and earth.

But let's say such arcane, aloof, impenetrable, uncommunicative, terror-inducing ghost exists. By what stretch of the imagination is *he* worthy of reverence, let alone love? *He* doesn't give a crap about his humble servants. And we are being asked to meekly bow and praise and worship *him* (or might *he* be a *she*?) and recoil in fear because we need to be reminded that we are part of something bigger than ourselves? The cosmos is infinitely bigger than we are. In fact, it's the biggest thing around. It's been eons since gullible, desperate savages looked at the starry vault, erected temples, sought its succor, begged to be blessed in battle, and pleaded for mercy when dying—none of which, neither they nor their descendants were ever granted. Haven't we learned anything? Are we too dumb to escape from the terminal collective psychosis that has us in its grip?

I invite those who disagree to refute my impudent assertions. In so doing, please put your Bible away, resist the impulse to quote the memorized slogans that were rammed down your throats, and just answer the *god-*damned question: Where is *god* when men weep, bleed, die? W H E R E ?

I'm not holding my breath.

◆ ◆ ◆

I can imagine tourists from another galaxy visiting a dried-up, dead Earth, finding the remnants of human civilizations, and remarking:

"These bi-pedal creatures must have had a great sense of humor. In the last five hundred years they transitioned from throwing children and vestal virgins into volcanoes to committing ecocide and killing each other as their imaginary spirits looked on."

◆ ◆ ◆

"When it comes to bullshit, big-time, major-league bullshit, you have to stand in awe of the all-time champion of false promises and exaggerated claims--religion. No contest. Religion easily has the greatest bullshit story ever told. Think about it. Religion has convinced people that there's an invisible man living in the sky who watches everything you do, every minute of every day. And the invisible man has a special list of ten things he does not want you to do. And if you do any of these ten things, he has a special place, full of fire and smoke and burning and torture and anguish, where he will send you to live and suffer and burn and choke and

scream and cry forever and ever 'til the end of time! But he loves you."
— George Carlin (1937-2008)

◆◆◆

"There is no attribute of god which is not either borrowed from the passions and powers of the human mind, or which is not a negation. Omniscience, Omnipotence, Omnipresence, Immutability, Incomprehensibility, and Immateriality ae all words that designate properties and powers peculiar to organized beings, with the addition of negations, by the idea of limitation is excluded."
—Percy Bysshe Shelley (1792-1822)

◆◆◆

"Properly read, the Bible is the most potent force for atheism ever conceived."
—Isaac Asimov (1920-1992)

◆◆◆

"What can be asserted without evidence can also be dismissed without evidence."
—Christopher Hitchens (1949-2011)

TRIBUTES

This book was conceived long before I set out to construct it piece by piece from a patchwork of childhood reminiscences, random musings hastily recorded on a pad in the dead of night, and simmering emotions spiced up by the steady pace of history endlessly retold. Several life-altering events and a harvest of images and insights gleaned during my years as an itinerant journalist also contributed to its protracted and painful gestation.

I must confess that when I decided to give this project wings, I was seduced by the notion that I would be penning the book I always wanted to read—an irreverent, vexing polemic, part exposé, part history part satire, part plausible conjecture—a tract that could somehow help galvanize a world mired in myth and sanctified deception. Fighting windmills, as the Man of la Mancha noted after two, maybe three valiant but impossible quests, is pointless. The *giants* of blind faith, conformity, and entrenched traditions are formidable foes, and common sense is swiftly submerged in the quicksand of ideological rigidity and fanaticism.

As I reviewed the manuscript one last time in search of stray typos and skewed syntax, I was reminded, as the French saying concludes, that *"Everything passes, everything breaks down, everything exhausts."* Everything includes anything that time renders irrelevant, including this unexceptional but candid work. I had no illusions about its utility or merit. I just kept going.

◆ ◆ ◆

I am indebted first and foremost to my parents, learned, urbane, open-minded, for instilling a love of books, music, art, philosophy, and science, for sparing me the enslavement of religious indoctrination—which, I am convinced, irreparably mutilates many children emotionally—and for enduring, if not always endorsing, my wildest escapades. To my mother, a selfless, unassuming, cultured woman of great refinement who insisted that human nature corrupts humans, I owe my reverence for beauty and symmetry, and my love of animals. From my father, a caring, iron-willed, and incorruptible man who abhorred ostentation and pretense, I learned that self-esteem and respect for truth confer infinitely greater gifts than money, material comfort, or celebrity.

I salute my teachers, those I pleased when I applied myself and those I exasperated. Their erudition, pedagogical skills, and saintly patience for the lazy, unfocused, mercurial, and rebellious student I was helped lay the foundations on which I would erect a lifetime career of endless beginnings.

I can never sufficiently acknowledge the immense influence several writers, poets, and philosophers have had on the constantly evolving person I would become and, by extension, on the ideas I would champion. Their prose, verses, insights, and eye-opening reflections resonate as intensely today as they did in the days of my youth. Most were French. One was denied a Christian funeral for penning vitriolic anti-clerical tracts. Four were imprisoned, the first for denouncing the bestiality of colonialism; the second—the son of a prostitute—for vagabondage, lewd acts, and *other offenses against public decency*; the third for stretching the limits of literary freedom in pamphlets that mixed raw eroticism with civil disobedience. The fourth spoke for the common man and rose with uncommon bravery against the profligacy of the clergy and the decadence of the military establishment.

Three were Russian. One of them, a novelist, essayist, and journalist, explored human psychology in the social, political, and spiritual milieu of his time. His works are populated with neurotics and lunatics, the kind who become pope, king, dictator, tyrant, president. It took as deranged a genius like him to understand and paint the frailties, aberrations, and horrors of life. Reading him is like descending into a snake pit of insanity. The poor man had epilepsy. He was sentenced to death for writing anti-tsarist tracts (the sentence was commuted at the last moment). He spent four years in a Siberian prison camp, followed by six years of compulsory military service in exile—enough to madden anyone. The second, a ruthless satirist, imparts surrealism and the grotesque with an unusual aura of normality. The third, the one that shocked me to my core, was a professional revolutionary, and theorist of anarchism. The man, an odious antisemite, was a closet authoritarian who condoned violence. I did agree with him when he remarked, *"Everything will pass, and the world will perish but* [Beethoven's] *Ninth Symphony will endure forever."*

My other mentors wrote in Arabic, English, Dutch, German, Sanskrit, and Spanish. Three hailed from Ireland. One did not survive the spurious puritanism of his Victorian milieu. The other died insane—as do those who seek shelter from the battering storm of reality in the sanctuary of delirium. The third was excommunicated for trying to resolve the conflict between religious dogma and secular knowledge, and for highlighting the depth of human ignorance. All were freethinkers, iconoclasts, rebels, defenders of secularism, all deceased, but whose heterodoxy and reformist ideas still inspire new generations of resisters, heroes, and martyrs.

It is with equal reverence that I thank my friends, few as they are, attentive and loyal, whose encouragement helped immensely as I battled illness, introspection, and self-criticism during the gestation of this and other works. I must also credit my detractors, far more numerous, for reinforcing my conviction that in this era of lies and unreason all opinions have equal weight but that only the truth, scarce but all-seeing and easily distorted, unnerving and often cruel, must prevail. Sadly, the evanescent nature of history's impact on succeeding generations does not include a built-in sense of anticipation for the horrors to come.

◆

◆   ◆

Born in Paris, W. E. Gutman is a retired
journalist, published author, and an atheist.
From 1994 to 2006, he reported from
Central America where he covered politics,
human rights, and other socio-economic
issues.

www.ingramcontent.com/pod-product-compliance
Lightning Source LLC
Chambersburg PA
CBHW022023090426
42739CB00006BA/254